WITHDRAWN

SPORTSEX

D1026387

SPORTSEX

Toby Miller

 Temple University Press

PHILADELPHIA

Temple University Press, Philadelphia 19122
Copyright © 2001 by Temple University
All rights reserved
Published 2001
Printed in the United States of America

⊖ The paper used in this publication meets the requirements of the
American National Standard for Information Sciences—Permanence
of Paper for Printed Library Materials, ANSI Z39.48-1984

Library of Congress Cataloging-in-Publication Data

Miller, Toby,
   Sportsex / Toby Miller.
      p.   cm.
   Includes bibliographical references (p.) and index.
   ISBN 1-56639-864-9 (cloth : alk. paper)—ISBN 1-56639-994-7 (pbk. : alk. paper)
      1. Sports—Anthropological aspects.   2. Gender identity.
   3. Sports—Social aspects.   I. Title.

GV706.2 M55 2001
306.4'83–dc21   00-049098

Contents

Acknowledgments

n writing this book, I have been conscious of a variety of potential audiences: folks who like sports but desire a critical account of its cultural politics; people who dislike sports and wish for the same criticism; readers who have an academic background in sports and sex through sociology or gender studies; and those who approach the topic from a cultural-studies perspective. Many discourses from these quarters are drawn upon in this volume, and I have several fellow travelers to thank for opening me up to them, starting with the co-authors of two chapters: Jim McKay, Randy Martin, and David Rowe. For comments on various parts of the book, I thank Ann Hall, Jason King, Micah Kleit, Geoffrey Lawrence, Marie Leger, Jim McKay, Susan Maier, Michael Messner, David Rowe, Don Sabo, and Sidonie Smith. For being the first to say I should write about sports, I thank Noel King. For encouraging my work on these topics in a variety of ways, I also wish to acknowledge Cheryl Cole, Faye Ginsburg, David Theo Goldberg, Lisa Henderson, Mary Jo Kane, May Joseph, Peter Labella, Chris Straayer, Alan Tomlinson, and Larry Wenner. For sharing my own bizarre world of exercise at different times, I thank Danny Anisfield,

Sarah Berry, Stuart Cunningham, Jock Given, Natalie Hirniak, Marie Leger, Randy Martin, Jim McKay, Jennifer Moore, Dan Mulhall, and Stephanie Tchan, and co-workers from the Department of Housing and Construction in Sydney and the central office of the Department of Employment and Industrial Relations in the early 1980s. To the coaches whom I write about in the introduction: Those still with us know who you are, and *I* know you'll never read this, but to hell with you anyway.

Some of the material in this book has appeared before, in versions that have been extensively revised here. Earlier venues were: *SportCult*, ed. Randy Martin and Toby Miller (University of Minnesota Press, 1999); Stuart Cunningham and Toby Miller, *Contemporary Australian Television* (University of New South Wales Press, 1994); *International Review for the Sociology of Sport* (1998); *Tourism, Leisure, Sport: Critical Perspectives*, ed. David Rowe and Geoffrey Lawrence (Cambridge University Press, 1998); *Journal of Sport and Social Issues* (1998); *The Olympics at the Millennium: Power, Politics, and the Games*, ed. Kay Schaffer and Sidonie Smith (Rutgers University Press, 2000); *Sport and Leisure: Trends in Australian Popular Culture*, ed. David Rowe and Geoff Lawrence (Harcourt Brace Jovanovich, 1990); *Men, Masculinities, and Sport*, ed. Jim McKay, Michael Messner, and Donald Sabo (Sage, 2000); and *Women and Performance: A Journal of Feminist Theory* (1999). I have also delivered related papers to the Australian Teachers of the Media (1988); the *Social Text* collective (1995); the Justice Studies program at Arizona State University (1997); the International Communication Association (1999); Unit One of Allen Hall at the University of Illinois, Champaign-Urbana (1999); and the English Department of the University of Queensland (1999). Thanks to those involved.

SPORTSEX

Introduction

Sportsextro

oving or hating sports has established a crucial divide between and among intellectuals and others. When I first started delivering papers about sports and gender more than a decade ago, this division emerged in audiences along gendered lines in a way that no longer holds true. In the 1980s, it seemed necessary to apologize to the cultural left for talking about this subject— now it is not. This is partly due to the spread of popular culture as an object of interest across the academy and partly to changes in advertising's political economy of looking and purchase. So it may seem anachronistic to revisit ambivalence about a critical investigation of sports. Yet I begin with a couple of stories that do just that. There are two reasons for doing this. First, these stories declare an ambiguous but distinct investment in the topic. Second, they model the ambivalence to come. This ambivalence has to do with unintended, potentially progressive, consequences of the capitalist marketing alluded to earlier. For while I welcome changes in cultural political economy that shift gender relations, I do so with profound caution. New forms of consumerism do not facilitate a wholesale democratic

1

cultural transformation—that would take more profound shifts in global economic politics and religion. But the new consumerism is generating a sea change in gender norms that is principally evident in sports. And this change seems too important to be left aside because it is not "real" politics or because it is occurring in a loved, or hated, sphere. Hence the book you now hold before you, and hence the two stories I am about to tell.

Story One

The athlete is already a being who has hypertrophized one organ, who turns his body into the seat and exclusive source of a continuous play. The athlete is a monster, he is the Man Who Laughs, the geisha with the compressed and atrophied foot, dedicated to total instrumentalization. —Umberto Eco (1987 [1969])

There are many reasons to loathe sports, and I've known a lot of them. My experience is probably quite typical. I had a brief literary introduction to sports from my father when he gave me a book about cricket. And sometimes we played the game together. I was enchanted by the heroism and grace in the book and the interaction in the garden. But that all changed.

Once these qualities became part of a disciplinary regime of brutality and negativity at school, they were forever compromised. In place of dashing, decent men working together to produce acts of beauty, I spent endless cold days wandering around rugby fields, being hit and kicked by opponents and shouted at by their parents, who bayed for blood. "Kill the Protestants" was a typical Catholic mother's refrain, and vice versa—a sectarian imprint on the well-worn tracks of vicarious surrogacy imposed by underachieving parents. We were nine years old. At home, my mother would seize my fingers every Saturday morning and apply her cuticle remover and tools as punishment for not having concentrated enough on the field earlier in the day. When sports wasn't about compulsory after-school activity, it meant gym work, which saw fascistic physical-education teachers standing over us, giving instruction in painful and pointless activities we never saw them deign to undertake—an early encouragement toward Maoism and participant observation! Sometimes we'd be lined up on the oval in our khaki uniforms to march—preparation for the cadet corps in high school and, later, the draft, "to fight communism and the Asian invasion."

I'm writing here about Australian and English schools of the 1960s and 1970s. These were fee-paying, all-male, WASP sites for the social reproduction of elites. Students were instructed to avoid people from government-funded schools at social events and on public transportation and were repeatedly reassured (though it always felt more like a threat) that we were destined to become "leaders of society." God knows what my fellow monsters became. This period also instilled fear of unwanted sexual advances in me—one of my instructors in English and fencing regularly forced us on an individual basis to strip and be beaten. This visibly and audibly excited him, and he added verbal humiliations. The rugby union and classics instructor rejoiced in shouting into my ear, from about six inches away, "Are you stupid or are you lying, Miller?" He also laughed at us on the field. The science-fiction and phys-ical-education instructor took special delight one afternoon when he required me to continue pole-vaulting and high-jumping after I had broken my wrist in front of him two minutes before. (No doubt he thought I was faking.)

My stories are nothing compared with others we have all heard. I got off lightly—as someone who was no good at sports, I was basically left alone to look inadequate, a nonentity. Of course, the laughs were not all on the side of these pathetic older men. We hated them with a passion, as well we might, and privately mocked their inane expressions of force. I was also lucky in that many jocks liked me—not least because, unlike my fellow incom-petents, I appreciated spectator sports and even enjoyed playing, provided there was no formal competition and I was among friends who were in it for fun and the expression of effort and skill rather than the pulverizingly dull desire to win at the expense of others.

And there lies the secret of something alongside my hatred of sports: the thrill when someone passes a football expertly and you run onto it; the sensation of receiving a hard-hit stroke and using its strength to return the ball to your colleague; the fun of running alongside others; and the pleasure of swimming in a creek with friends. Adrienne Rich (1997) refers to this as "what makes the body shoot . . . into its pure and irresistible curve." Such joys are quite distant from the horror-show world of competition, authority, and critique that characterized the ritual humiliation of schooldays. At the same time, this notion of transcendence has itself been commodified and romanticized: The clichés I deployed earlier could have come from a Nike advertisement or the gung-ho alibis of sports disciplinarians. Part of the reason for the success of these tropes is that they reference the work of both players and spectators, the excitement that can transcend the capitalist complex of sports—even as this transcendence is the promise on which that commodification is founded.

Sports embodies the distinction between a world of domination, scientific management, and an artificially generated dislike of others, and a world of collaboration, spontaneity, and fellowship. These are the "bad" and the "good" of sports, what I hate and what I love. My specific memories of coaches form a small part of a mosaic. In the case of that particular class, gender, and racial experience, they have a terrible legacy, of course. This legacy connects practices of power and knowledge to control of a domestic proletariat, to misogyny, and to colonialism. We must never forget this history and what it still symbolizes, produces, and governs. One example came in AT&T's 1999 campaign to win the local U.S. telephone market. The company advertised itself by playing with memories of childhood. A blurred graphic of children sprinting, captioned "Remember racing with your friends?" was offset with "Competition helped everyone run faster."[1] Perhaps, but it made me shy away, as does its metaphorization in the service of capital. At the same time, when tempted to express disdain for the banal competitiveness and disciplinary obsessions of sports, the untrammeled ecstasy of catching a wave or seeing someone else do so is a perfect utopian alternative to this seemingly most capitalistic of metaphors.

And this alternative can be realized at improbable moments because of sports' high allegorical value and nostalgia quotient. CBS television's coverage of the 1997 U.S. Open Tennis Final included footage of Arthur Ashe. I remember the interest in Australia when he won the 1968 Open—not because he was an African American in a predominantly white sport, but because we were astonished that any American could win a Grand Slam. A few years later, with new global powers in tennis displacing Australia, Ashe was up against the apotheosis of arrogant white masculinity—Jimmy Connors—in a Wimbledon final. (Remember those bloated white guys in the expensive seats at any number of U.S. tournaments, rising to punch the air in mimesis of his juvenilia?) Our exhilaration that Ashe's subtle variations and skill won the day was enormous. When his heart condition was revealed, and when he died so young, those traumas combined with his ability, philanthropy, and vision to leave the legacy of a cultural hero.

On this day in 1997, CBS's montage sequence included a shot of Ashe on the court, joking and laughing with Bobby Kennedy. I hate to join the ranks of romantic bores/boors raving about lost possibilities of the '60s. But this moment of hope reminded me that sports and youth culture do not have to be aggressive, dismissive, or "pumped up" to be progressive and the best. At the same time, seeing those men together is a reminder of trauma: the Americans and Australians in Vietnam and Kennedy's stance on ending the war; AIDS and Ashe's infection and death; and the stalled momentum of the civil-rights movement following the assassinations of '68, all brought together and nostalgically memorialized in sports.

The paradox at the heart of sports—their simultaneously transcendent and imprisoning qualities and their astonishing capacity to allegorize—is most obvious, dangerous, and transformative in its gendered form. Sports have long been regarded as a "masculine preserve," where men can congregate as men without women to assist in their definition as people.[2] Sports are frequently criticized as a "resonant symbol of masculine hegemony," because they superficially "embod[y] the natural superiority of men over women," despite the fact that sporting capacity is rarely readable through size.[3] A brutality toward the self is there, too, as per Alan Klein's ethnographic findings:

> The first time I witnessed a bodybuilder suffer a nosebleed while lifting weights it was triumphantly explained to me that the man in question was a true bodybuilder, paying dues, training in earnest and willing both to risk and to endure injury for his calling. Sometime later, when I watched another bodybuilder doubled over in pain from what would later be diagnosed as a symptom of hepatic tumors on the liver, it was again interpreted by the behemoths in the gym as testimony to his commitment to the subculture. In both cases I watched men reinterpret signs of clear and present danger to their health as ringing endorsements of character.[4]

But accounts of sports as an exclusive zone of male privilege are not tenable. When the legendary homophobic, Christian Green Bay Packers tight end Reggie White writes an op-ed piece for the *Wall Street Journal* protesting "female reporters and camerawomen ogling guys in the locker room," as he did in 1999, and the *New York Times* notes that 160 of the country's 900 male jockeys have been treated for substance abuse as they have tried to make their bodies weigh less than 117 pounds, we know that change is afoot and contradictions are aplenty in sports and gender.[5] It is not just women who are objects of the gaze; it is not just women who are physically damaged in the interests of social expectations; and it is not just men who are invigilating the bodies of others:

> The discourse on sports is like no other in our culture insofar as its object is the male body; its currency is statistical comparison of performances, of exchange rates and ownership, of strategies for deployment of bodies, and of the particular weaknesses, quirks, and gradual submission to injury, illness, and aging of those bodies. At the center of this discourse is an image of fascination, the perfect machine of a body-in-motion choreographed with others as a vision of grace and power: "Now, there's an athlete!"[6]

Ambivalence lies at the heart of this book. For in the two decades between Ashe's Grand Slam victory and his death, professional men's sports were transformed into an internationalist capitalist project. As part of the desire to address TV spectators and capture their attention for advertisers, the male body became an object of lyrical rhapsody and the gaze of the other. In keeping with that shift, *Sportsex* analyzes masculinity not as a property or essence, but as contingent signs and practices.

These signs exercise power over both men and women. Paul Smith says that "masculinity isn't always a pleasant thing to behold, and it's always difficult, sometimes unpleasant to write about—it's certainly a difficult thing in just about every respect."[7] Through analyzing this "unpleasantness," I have found evidence of transformation, not stasis, and that animates the chapters to come.

Story Two

When he [my father] sat down at the television to watch a baseball game, volume blaring, cigar smoke wafting across the room (or a wet, extinguished butt in the ashtray, sending off its acrid fumes), it seemed that he owned our collective space absolutely. . . . Even today, I can't listen to the sounds of a televised sports event without feeling irritated, and vaguely queasy. —Susan Bordo (1998, 10)

My friend Rob Nixon and I watched the 1998 men's World Cup soccer match between Colombia and England in a lower-west-side Manhattan nightclub that had opened its daytime doors to soccer fans. The crowd was English. The man next to me was wearing a T-shirt that identified him as someone from a working-class area of London. His voice went with it. We never spoke, but he clutched at me whenever England did well and embraced me with each goal and the ultimate victory. Initially uncomfortable, I found myself looking forward to these shows of emotion. That encounter made me think about the masculinities on display in the competition, the strange gamut of passions and passionate exchanges—players blowing kisses, driving one another into the ground with projectile cuddles, and adopting strange poses for the crowd, for all the world like fey, queer-acting models. (Think of Michael Laudrup celebrating his goal for Denmark against Brazil.)

Our location embodied this change. The sports bar has undergone massive gentrification and feminization. From its 1940s origins as a TV added to the tavern in order to bring men back out of the home, the sports bar evolved into a male-dominated sphere until its dramatic transformation in the 1990s. Whereas the old single-set and long bar live on in a few venues, the dominant "postmodern sports bar," as Lawrence Wenner has called it, "is an extension of domesticated mall design," with an emphasis on cleanliness, multiple TVs and sites for viewing, diverse satellite signals, airiness, and a successful appeal to female customers.[8] No surprise, then, that my friend and I should be in the millennial incarnation of "Nell's," one of the hottest New York bars since the '80s, and not generally thought of as a masculinist or sports venue.

Those who saw the wonderful England–Argentina World Cup game may have followed later denunciations of David Beckham, the brilliant midfielder who had helped win the Colombia match but this time was sent from the field for retaliating against a foul. That left his team a player down, and they went on to lose. The reaction in Britain was predictable, with lynchings threatened and the usual Fleet Street atrocities.

On the morning of the match, prior to Beckham's dismissal, the egregious Rupert Murdoch's equally egregious newspaper, *The Sun,* had depicted Beckham as Eva Peron, perhaps because he had recently been photographed at a party in France dressed in a sarong with his affianced, Posh Spice (yes), on his arm. So the knives were out before his mistake—and this clearly had to do with questions of masculinity and patriotism. Beckham was punished for being pretty and flash. His looks, his style, and his sex life feminized him for the British tabloid papers and parts of the public. This was his crime—to be on the edge of conventional manliness. Throughout the next two domestic seasons, Beckham was taunted by crowds throughout England, who queered his masculinity. Yet he was also a high-profile commodity, appearing, for example, on the cover of London's *Time Out* magazine depicted as Christ and fielding questions about anal sex in an accompanying interview. This attention depended on his looks and sexual aura. Similarly, Oscar de la Hoya's defeat in a 1999 world-title boxing defense was seen in some quarters as a moral punishment. Well ahead on points, de la Hoya, whose appeal rests on beautiful style and beautiful looks, elected to move away from his opponent in the closing rounds, lest he be hit hard. The controversial decision against him was thought to have been a punitive reaction to this "unmanliness."

Clearly, repressive gender conventions are some of the first memories we have of sports. But the brutal deindustrialization that has cut the underpinnings of First World working-class masculinity has also seen a dramatic shift of capital into the service sector, with sports a huge part of the entertainment complex that is a cradle of First World wealth. Beauty is as much a part of male sports discourse today as toughness, while grace is the avowed compatriot of violence. These antinomies have always enjoyed frottage on the field, but their relationship has become crucial to marketing both individuals and sports itself in ways that were occasional and casual in earlier times. Sports have become governed not by administrators *tout court*, but by venture capitalists, with the body their target. Governmentality—the refinement of human bodies through rationalization and utilitarianism—connects to capital accumulation in a dispersed network of power that cannot be explained in terms of a unilinear connection between all sports and all laboring and consuming forces. It is equally driven by the search for individual health and happiness via the conditioned and consuming body, sex appeal, and self-discipline.

Spectator sports reference all the complexities of contemporary capitalism, played out over the public bodies of headlined workers. Sports' gender politics at the elite level today are far from a functionalist world of total domination by straight, orthodox masculinity because of the niche targets that these commodified signs are directed toward (such as straight women and gay men). There is, of course, a regressive side to commodification and its reproduction of heroism, because they displace public attention from structural social inequalities. We are all too familiar with the claims of corporate feminism about social change. But the beneficial aspect to cataloguing sports is its challenges to gender convention. For example, Calistoga bottled water was advertised in the official program of the 1994 Gay Games with the slogan: "We don't label people. Just bottles." Such corporations have seen potential profit in supporting fringe actors and activities in sport, ameliorating the chauvinism of traditional amateur-games bodies. Adidas realized long before the International Olympic Committee (IOC) did that emerging sovereign states should be courted. The company dedicated resources in the '70s to forwarding the claims of African and Central European sports federations, and drew a consequent reward—in addition to free advertising—when sporting attire was selected to outfit teams. From the very first days of women's activism for access to marathons in the 1960s, Avon tied its door-to-door globalization strategies to the struggle, funding races, hiring lobbyists, and connecting the sport to beauty and makeup. (This support is contingent, of course. The company felt very differently about lesbians' involvement, cutting sponsorship of women's tennis after the 1981 "galimony" suit against Billie Jean King.) Avon sponsors the U.S. Olympic Team as part of its bizarre

"Avon Salutes the Woman Inside the Athlete" campaign. A double-page spread in *Vanity Fair*'s issue on the 1996 Olympic Games in Atlanta invited readers to look at an image of an elderly woman in evening wear surrounded by four swimsuited young men and "guess which one's the Olympic gold medalist in springboard diving." The answer was Aileen Riggin Soule, who had won the event in 1920. She was described in bold type as "just another Avon lady." Nike learned the lesson: A 1990s female-empowerment campaign sent sales to women up 40 percent.[9]

These challenges and inconsistencies in the sight of heightened commodification make sports exciting at an analytic and political level. Clearly, sports continue to be a space of heteronormative, masculinist, and white power, but they are undergoing immense change, with sex at the center. Objectification is a fact of sexual practice within capitalism.[10] Excoriating evaluation of women's bodies has long been the pivotal node of this process, with the implied spectator a straight male. Now, slowly in many cases but rapidly in others, the process of body commodification through niche targeting has identified men's bodies as objects of desire and gay men and straight women as consumers, while there are signs of targeting lesbian desire. Masculinity, understood as a set of dominant practices of gendered power, is no longer the exclusive province of men as spectators, consumers, or agents. "Female masculinity" can now be rearticulated as a prize rather than a curse,[11] and the longstanding ambiguity of macho sportsmen dressing in drag has become a point-of-sale rather than a suds-laden moment of excess.

This is especially striking given that the United States has not traditionally gone in for "humorous" sports cross-dressing in the way that many Anglo societies have done. Today, the retired track star Carl Lewis appears in fuck-me pumps for Pirelli tires, a company traditionally associated with calendars of heteronormative women; the New York Knicks forward Larry Johnson sells Converse products dressed up as his grandmother; the Ottawa Senators rookie

Alexander Daigle poses as a female nurse for trading cards; the world-champion boxer Chris Eubank models a Vivienne Westwood frock on Milanese catwalks; the lapsed power forward Dennis Rodman wears a white wedding gown to his book signing; and the Thai kickboxer Pirinya Kiatbusaba uses his purses to fund transsexual surgery. The former New York Jets quarterback Joe Namath is still renowned for pitching Hanes pantyhose in the 1970s.[12] Of course, there are misogynistic aspects to drag of this kind, but it is a new and burgeoning practice that suggests other changes, as well.

I do not celebrate these changes unproblematically. Our conjuncture continues to be one where, for example, invisible and unpaid women's work, such as ferrying players, mending uniforms, and so on, is the sine qua non of most sport, while men's power over women continues.[13] But a decade ago, Beverley Poynton noted that this invisibility extended to fandom—female spectators were excluded "from the discourse of football" in their voyeurism, as well as in their emotional and physical labor.[14] Since then, changes have come. The American Dialect Society decreed "soccer mom" its 1996 Word of the Year, as politicians vied for electoral support from middle-class women who drove children and men across the country.[15] In 1999, David Letterman troped the term when he coined the expression "Soccer Mamas" for the World Cup winners—both sexy and maternal now. In the mid-1990s, National Football League (NFL) administrators discerned a threat to the game's man appeal from other media forms and faced mothers who objected to their sons' playing so mindlessly violent a sport. The NFL responded by hiring Sara Levinson to run marketing—the first woman to be employed in the league's central-office executive group in a position other than secretary. Levinson was selected because her previous job had been co-president of MTV. The NFL wanted her to push merchandising spinoffs and attract female audiences. This became known as the "Women's Initiative," named because "our research indicates that women like the tight pants on the players." Co-educational high-school football was introduced, along with Levinson's new argot, which talked of the NFL as a brand, not as something quasi-holy.[16] NFL broadcasters are employing more and more female announcers and experts to cater to the increasing numbers of women watching on TV in response to the feminizing initiatives taken over the past five years.[17] Meanwhile, male players were complaining about the ritual objectification of standing near-naked as hundreds of administrators, owners, coaches, medics, scouts, and other men calibrated their bodies at meat-market conventions.[18] Somewhere across town, female wrestlers in the United States make big money from telephone and apartment wrestling, simulating bouts with male callers or visiting them for the real thing. These workers do not see themselves as part of the sex industry, despite the semiotic similarities.[19]

How should we make sense of these developments? Just as the bourgeoisie has managed to be the most revolutionary class in history, so its means of reification, in all its sophistication, has had both beneficial and baleful consequences. Gerald Early quotes a contemporary boxing manager describing his sport as "capitalism gone crazy."[20] That "craziness" is undercutting crucial aspects of patriarchal relations in a series of limit cases that I investigate in this book.

After the 1999 Women's World Cup of Soccer, the *New York Times* journalist Richard Lipsyte wrote a column entitled "Sports and Sex Are Always Together." In it he argued that "sexuality may be so intrinsic to sports that unless the audience is sexually comfortable, the game just won't sell." Despite a few pieties about gender and commodification, Lipsyte fancied this aspect to the game: "I say the more flesh the better." A week later, his column offered a pseudo-apology after significant public criticism.[21] Both the initial claim and the powerful reaction to it are pointers to the Sportsex *Geist:* The present moment of change is a radical one, and I guardedly welcome it. Sportsex is everywhere—sold as such. It is both intensely discriminating in its identification of commodities and consumers and increasingly attuned to difference. A truly progressive politics that will transform the labor process? That would take another revolution, from a different class. For the moment, the urgent drive toward the creation of markets to deal with overproduction has turned the Sportsex body to the forefront of contemporary capitalism. It is both a sign and a source of social change.

1

Bodnam
Body, Nation, Media

Body

Why are lesbians so drawn to sports? One would have to be stupid (or straight) not to notice that there are lots of us out there on America's softball fields, volleyball courts, golf courses, bowling alleys, and—current hotbed—karate dojos. . . . Even before my heart raced for a woman, it raced for gym class. It was the happiest part of my day, the physical exertion, the camaraderie, and the emotional intensity that was part of team-bonding. And who didn't have a crush on a coach? I've never met a lover in a bar, but I have met several on the squash court. —*Susan Reed (1994, 20), senior writer,* People *magazine*

The body is "an emblem of society." No longer a sidebar to the study of society and culture, the body must now line up front and center, with sports a key site for analysis and intervention, of social and cultural contestation. Bodily discourses of exertion, force, rules, and competition provoke struggles between dominant and subordinate groups for symbolic and material rewards.[1] Of course, more generally social control is exercised through bodily coercion and consent, by training bodies to discipline themselves into a quasi-mechanical way of life.[2] There are clear links between sports and this overall disciplinary process. Objectifying analogies

15

between the sporting body and the machine are exemplified in BMW's 1996 line of cars. A company catalog describes these vehicles as "athletes of grace, power and championship performance," built in "the spirit of the Olympic Games."

In their elite commercial form, sports have reflected and projected a worldwide "body panic" as well as a functionalist system of reification.[3] The subversion of traditional gender-bound body images; the emergence of HIV and AIDS; and the expansion of bodily surveillance, commodification, and manipulation have problematized bodies in new ways across 1990s America. So Dennis Rodman appears on the basketball court with multiple earrings, multicolored hair, and a queer persona. Amy Acuff, frustrated that her consistently brilliant high-jumping over five years has not generated media or public attention, competes in a fur halter top and fur-lined bikini pants, then gathers top female athletes together to create a nude calendar for 2000. And Anne Langstaff, veteran ultra-marathoner and topless dancer, is sponsored to run by her nighttime employer, Dreamgirls of San Diego.[4]

These are limit cases of a wider phenomenon. For with the advent of consumer capitalism and postmodern culture, the body has become an increasingly visible locus of desire. The manipulation of appearance through fashion codes, bodily adornment, calculated nutrition, and physical-conditioning regimes has projected body images into the social realm with renewed importance.[5] Bodies are both subjects and objects, active phenomena that are also acted upon in the social: "People make their bodies through labour, sport and play, but they do not make them in circumstances of their own choosing."[6] Physical, psychic, and representational bodies become meaningful through "corporeal subjectivities ... there is no monolithic category 'the body' ... only particular kinds of bodies."[7] Sports are a privileged site for defining, altering, and monitoring these subjectivities, and important structural homologies and allegorical implications articulate sports with sex.

The sporting body and sex have always been bracketed, by eros, government, or science. In ancient Greece and Rome, the body was the locus for an ethics of the self, a combat with pleasure and pain that enabled people to find the truth about themselves and master their drives.[8] Austerity and hedonism could be combined through training: "The metaphor of the match, of athletic competition and battle, did not serve merely to designate the nature of the relationship one had with desires and pleasures, with their force that was always liable to turn seditious or rebellious; it also related to the preparation that enabled one to withstand such a confrontation."[9]

Xenophon, Socrates, and Diogenes held that sexual excess and decadence came from the equivalent of sporting success. In sex and sports, triumph could lead to failure unless accompanied by regular examination of the conscience and physical training. Carefully modulated desire in both spheres became a sign of fitness to govern others. Aristotle and Plato favored regular, ongoing flirtations with excess, as tests and as pleasures. This ethos was distinctly gendered: The capacity of young men to move into positions of social responsibility was judged by their skill at charioteering and managing men; their ability to win "the little sports drama" was akin to dealing with sexually predatory older men.[10]

Five hundred years later, the sexual ethics of ancient Rome attached anxieties to the body and sport. Spirituality had emerged to complicate exercises of the self as a means of training for governance:

> The increased medical involvement in the cultivation of the self appears to have been expressed through a particular and intense form of attention to the body. This attention is very different from that manifested by the positive valuation of physical vigor during an epoch when gymnastics and athletic and military training were an integral part of the education of a free man. Moreover, it has something paradoxical about it since it is inscribed, at least in part, within an ethics that posits that death, disease, or

even physical suffering do not constitute true ills and that it is better to take pains over one's soul than to devote one's care to the maintenance of the body. But in fact the focus of attention in these practices of the self is the point where the ills of the body and those of the soul can communicate with one another and exchange their distresses; where the bad habits of the soul can entail physical miseries, while the excesses of the body manifest and maintain the failings of the soul. . . . The body the adult has to care for, when he is concerned about himself, is no longer the young body that needed shaping by gymnastics; it is a fragile, threatened body, undermined by petty miseries.[11]

In place of personal excesses, which had preoccupied Athens in the fourth century B.C., Rome in the first century A.D. was principally concerned with frailty—the finitude of life and fitness. Moral arguments were imbued with "nature and reason," and exercises of the self joined this more elevated search for truth.[12] These homologies have spread across the globe with the rise of public education. Today, most young people living in industrialized societies are subject to bodily and ethical regimes that equate body and mind: a visual economy of public and private sites.

This economy came into being at the uneasy nineteenth-century encounter of industrial modernity, auto- and homoeroticism and sociality, and pastoral nostalgia, a space where a capitalist division of labor and new technology meet, and science, myth, and religion pronounce upon the sexed sports body. Jon Stratton connects sexuality to sporting vigor, with desire simulated through work and spiritual uplift: Corporal Hitler meets Cardinal Newman and Lord Reith on Eton fields. This reached its apogee in the nineteenth century at Oxbridge, where some colleges placed a premium on sports over academic performance. Empire and nation became identified with men's team sports, perhaps an abiding reason that "coming out" seems easier in individual games, where the stakes of representativeness are lower.[13] In the 1890s, Oskar Zoth ingested liquid extracts from a bull's testicles to improve his cycling and swimming. The last

English Football Association Cup Final before the Second World War was allegedly won and lost on the strength of which team had taken monkey-gland tablets in training (the losers). Contemporary Indian wrestling ascetics constrain the flow of semen to exercise power and authority—celibacy and the mat. International cricket tours are famous for correlations drawn between the success of men's teams when they are not "distracted" by accompanying wives or girlfriends. We can all offer lists of great sporting achievements that followed nights of denial (Khalid Khannouchi's marathons, Muhammad Ali's fights, the successful 1996 Canadian Olympic swim team, Mike Ditka's Chicago Bears ["If wives and girlfriends can't wait, let them take a cold shower"], John Elway's Super Bowl victories) versus nights of indulgence (Wilt Chamberlain's 100-point basketball game, Bob Beamon's 1968 Olympic long jump, Brazil's 1994 World Cup of men's soccer victory, Kerrin-Lee Gartner's 1992 Olympic skiing gold, Marty Liquori's mile record, Joe Namath's Super Bowl victory). There have also been numerous reflections on unexpected defeats that led to problematizations of sexual practice (Mike Tyson blaming a boxing defeat in 1990 on too much sex, and the famous 1974 World Cup of men's soccer final between the Netherlands and the Federal Republic of Germany—the Dutch, instructed to have sex the night before, scored a goal in the first minute but flagged later; the Germans, instructed to abstain, scored two late goals). And after losing a 2000 European Championship qualifying match, five members of the Israeli soccer team were investigated on the grounds of having had sex before the game.[14] Following the Sydney Games, statistics were offered again and again on television to the effect that athletes had used 30,000 condoms during the two weeks of competition.

Anabolic-androgenic steroids that provide testosterone are central to sport. Steroids are officially proscribed by all international sporting authorities, are dangerous to the liver, and can cause cardiac damage and sexual problems. (The mad-weightlifter disease that reportedly sends users into "roid rage" is unconfirmed.) The Human Growth Hormone, which *Sports Illustrated* labeled "hormone of the moment" in 1997, disfigures cheekbones, jaws, and foreheads. Pressure to perform has led to its widespread use (see Chapter Three). The U.S. Department of Health reported that a quarter-million schoolboys were taking steroids in 1991, mostly in athletic programs, while almost all Olympic-competition track-and-field athletes in the United States appear to be involved. The number of teenage women using anabolics doubled to 175,000 in the 1990s, and about 3 million men in the United States are estimated to use them.[15]

How might we make sense of these trends theoretically and historically? Norbert Elias, who analyzes sports and social structure synchronically and diachronically, coined the term "figuration" to designate how people inhabit social positions. The figural keys to sport are exertion, contest, codification, and collective meaningfulness. Without these, the magic attractions of sports—tension and catharsis—cannot be guaranteed. Elias asks why there is such fascination with rule-governed contests between individuals and teams, evident in a trend that fans out from the European ruling classes after the sixteenth century. Sentiment and behavior are codified, supplanting excess and self-laceration with auto-critique. The displacement of tension and the search for ordered leisure allocate to organized sport the task of controlling and training gentry, workers, and colonists alike. High tension and low risk blend popular appeal with public safety—a utilitarian calculus of time and joy.[16] Of course, these trends are subject to local customization and struggle. Henning Eichberg points to contradictory, non-linear shifts in European sports between the thirteenth and nineteenth centuries, with enclosure and the open air in an ambiguous relationship.[17] The spatial separation of sports from nature in late-nineteenth-century industrialization marks a trend whereby bodies in motion are progressively contained, enraging hygiene movements but allowing surveillance, spectacle, and profit.

Following Elias, Joseph Maguire typifies the sporting body as a model of discipline, a mirror, a site of domination, and a form of communication. The disciplined body is remodeled through diet and training. The mirroring body functions as a machine of desire, encouraging mimetic conduct via the purchase of commodities. The dominating body exercises power through physical force, both on the field and—potentially—off it. Finally, the communicative body is an expressive totality, balletic and beautiful. These taxonomies bleed into one another and can be internally conflictual or straightforwardly functional. They are carried by human, commercial, and governmental practices that stretch and maintain boundaries among athletes, sporting performance, and aspiration. For instance, kinesiology, an instrumental and apolitical sports science, is committed to competition. Its measurement fetish provides Tayloristic evaluation and control.[18]

Just such instrumentalism stimulates lugubrious lamentations over lost transcendence. So Christopher Lasch sees contemporary American sport as a degraded version of what was once a beautiful "release from everyday life." This release was available thanks to a heightened, highly specific awareness that could be reached via intense concentration and a replication of childhood's singular obsessions. Twentieth-century social reformers sought to harness such energies to nation-building and economic productivity at the same time as capitalism was transforming sports into a practice of spectatorship.[19] Those twin pleasures—discipline and profiteering—"corrupted" sports' transcendent qualities. Lasch's critique is a romantic desire, shared by many on the left and the right, for what is lost when the body shifts from free play to lax consumption as the life world is commodified.

And Maguire's four types clearly reference a century of science applied to defining and differentiating masculinity and femininity. In the nineteenth century, it was thought that women could only bear healthy children if they exercised in moderation (picking up an anxiety dating back to sixteenth-century Europe that working out could transform women into men). With the emergence of sexology and internationally competitive sport in the twentieth century came panic over the very sex of athletes. Revisiting 1970s debates about the femininity of sportswomen, Judith Butler has pointed out the multiple irony of applied gender science from those days: that the oscillation in sex testing between chromosomal and hormonal signs registered both an anxiety to fix identity and the unattainability of acultural, ahistorical absolutes. This crisis of femininity is productive.[20]

Three discourses articulate science and gender through sport. Categorization labels certain physical and behavioral norms as male or female in terms of either nature or society. Activities coded as male are evaluated to see whether they "contaminate" female participants. Sex-role analysis accounts for differences in the uptake of sports by girls and boys through socialization. And androgyny studies "permit" intermingled behavior across gender. Against these social-psychology approaches, distributive critics emphasize inequalities of opportunity and power. A sociological model displaces a psychological one, but it remains a liberal position: As long as the preconditions are in place for equilibrium, whatever happens from that point is meant to be, with sports in need of equalization, not transformation. By contrast, the left problematizes the overall historical, social, economic, and cultural mythology of sports.[21]

The recent turn toward strong bodies as women's fashion statements, for all the associated rhetoric of empowerment, privileges a small and implausible array of somatotypes: "a body that is slim, tight, and small-breasted; a body that signifies deference through its posture, movements, and gestures; and a bodily surface disciplined for adornment." Marketed as "technologies of transgression," worked-out bodies are equally "normalizing technologies," with the body a self-styled and -nominated commodity and sign of sobriety that is nevertheless quite risky in terms of long-established gendered norms. A hermeneutics of suspicion surrounds this desirable body: Is it still female, is it still feminine, and is it drug-enhanced?[22]

Femininity's partner in instability, masculinity, also spreads its wears and troubles unevenly across sites. Sports have been a crucial site for training and expressing male violence, both on and off the field. This is evident from the record of domestic assault and public attacks on bystanders by athletes. It includes 56 professional U.S. football players charged with domestic violence between 1989 and 1994 (see Chapter Three) and high-profile murder charges arising from the 1999–2000 pro football season.[23] Michael Messner argues that:

> Football, based as it is on the most extreme possibilities of the male body ... is clearly a world apart from women, who are relegated to the role of cheerleaders/sex objects on the sidelines.... In contrast to the bare and vulnerable bodies of the cheerleaders, the armored bodies of the football players are elevated to mythical status, and as such, give testimony to the undeniable "fact" that here is at least one place where men are clearly superior to women.[24]

However, the capacity of sports to ideologize masculine superiority has been destabilized as women have struggled to gain greater access and commercially minded sports governors have sought women out as consumers. Increasing numbers of women are competing in traditionally male sports such as power lifting, bodybuilding, the martial arts, football, rugby, and ice hockey, and women often outperform men in stamina-based events. The year 2000 saw the formation of a Women's Professional Football League; Tonya Butler winning a football scholarship to junior college and successfully kicking extra points; and Laila Ali following in her father's career with several boxing knockouts.[25] These women's entry into customarily male preserves illustrates the "double movement of containment and resistance" that characterizes cultural struggles among dominant and subordinate groups.[26] On the one hand, the presence of vigorous and robust female athletes demonstrates that sporting prowess is not "naturally" masculine.

On the other, the presence of physically powerful women precipitates attempts by men to limit women's aspiration and resistance.[27] A paradox is at work in these "intrusions." Women's restricted access to sports has been sustained via biologistic claims that their bodies are unsuited to athletic activities. Now these old scientistic arguments function partially in reverse, thanks to women's superiority in certain endurance events. But just as antique scientism was vitally connected to power relations between the sexes, so latter-day biological "truth" is deeply encrusted with social politics in terms of access to facilities, training, and prestige.

Women were not admitted to track-and-field events at the Olympics until 1928, in response to a separatist event in 1922, and were not permitted to run farther than 200 meters at the games until 1960. The marathon and pole vault became legitimate for women only in the 1980s and '90s. The International Olympic Committee excluded women from its numbers until 1981. Although the 1996 Atlanta Olympiad saw a larger proportion of female competitors than ever before, women amounted to just 34 percent of all athletes, with men competing for 63 more medal events than women. Twenty-seven nations still decline to send female competitors, and international TV coverage excludes women's events from many Arabic eyes.[28] Forty-two percent of the athletes at the Olympics in Sydney were women, and they competed in the same number of team events as men.[29]

Just as men's organizations co-opted women's sports in the 1920s, the 1980s saw a repeat. Title IX of the 1972 U.S. Educational Amendment Act barred discrimination by gender in federally assisted teaching institutions. As a consequence, the representation of women in intercollegiate sports rose from just 9 percent of total numbers in 1966–67 to 32 percent in 1985–86, while women's participation at the high-school level rose 500 percent and the proportion of girls involved in high-school varsity sports grew from 1 in 27 in 1972 to 1 in 3 in 1999. But college sports budgets for women have not developed as they should.

What was designed to desegregate gender has seen men take over the senior administration and coaching of women's sports. Although the National Collegiate Athletic Association (NCAA) failed when it sought to reverse Title IX, it did lure colleges away from the Association for Intercollegiate Athletics for Women with the promise of media exposure and money. Prior to Title IX, 90 percent of the sports coaches at women's colleges were women. In 2000, the proportion was 45.6 percent, and the salaries of female head coaches of Division 1-A teams averaged just 63 percent of the salaries paid to male coaches in 1997. Put another way, women have more opportunities to play, but they also have unequal rewards and drastically reduced access to managerial power. We also see this reflected in professional coefficients of Title IX, such as the 1990s emergence of the Women's National Basketball Association (WNBA). By the end of the 1990s, the proportion of female coaches in the WNBA had dropped from 88 percent to 42 percent.[30]

On the textual front, women's bodily power has traditionally been claimed by orthodox representational norms. But while Olympic gymnastics inscribes bodily meanings onto women that tightly circumscribe beauty and femininity, it also presents a sustained challenge to conventional accounts of women's physical abilities. The competitive nature of international sports has of necessity extended the form and rigor of exercise beyond polite gender divisions. Activities that previously were restricted to male gymnasts are incorporated into women's routines, thereby equating strength with grace as a sign of competence in public performances, while the male figure skater Rudy Galindo performs routines containing elements that are coded as feminine (such as displaying his ass). All of this, however, occurs in an additionally contradictory manner: Juvenile female competitors are taught to flirt with their audiences in the quest for judge and crowd appeal. When Olga Korbut and Nadia Comaneci won a slew of Olympic gymnastics medals in 1972 and 1976, respectively, they also changed judging standards. Routines suited to the low fat ratios and flexible bodies of some girls in their very early teens became "required," leading to dietary disorders and crippling arthritis. What could be a celebration of flexibility, strength, and agility is a site for improbable desires and strictures, occasioned by norms of femininity that tie expressive totality to particular body shapes and practices. Female college gymnasts are six times as likely as other Americans to suffer anorexia or bulimia. Many contestants take "brake drugs"—substances used to diminish mens' sex drive—to reduce their growth and put their health at risk by "playing hurt."[31]

At the "other end" of femininity, women's college teams are regularly vilified by the media in sexualized language, and college coaches are known to begin the first practice of the year with the requirement that players not be "lesbian during the season." Despite the significant number of lesbians in the old Women's Professional Basketball League, "out" players were harassed and fired. Like Billie Jean King, the tennis champion Martina Navratilova lost major endorsements when her sexual practices became public, litigated knowledge in the 1980s (but was hawking Subarus on television in 2000).

Queerness is a major issue across genders. Sports allow men to watch and dissect other men's bodies in fetishistic detail, a space for staring without homosexuality alleged or feared. Sam Fussell describes muscles as "the latest props of the dandy." The fetish of admiring body parts ("look at those triceps") gives a scientistic pleasure and alibi. A man who is lifting weights gives off signs of pleasure–pain akin to facial correlatives of the male orgasm, a sight otherwise denied men who define themselves as straight. One lifter has said that a good pump is "better than coming"— no wonder turning tricks is as common in such gyms as the disavowal of homosexuality.[32]

In 1995, the U.S. Supreme Court ruled that people in sports changing rooms have a diminished right to privacy. Despite the fact that sports avowedly play up physicality and play down sexuality, the act and art of looking can cause problems. Paul Foss suggests "shower-room banter, that slightly nervous parading of one's personal capital before the other boys at school or after sport, never entirely leaves us when we finally grow up to learn that this is a forbidden subject."[33] But a less politically and personally dubious reading practice is available, as well: For the gay man in 1950s Britain who was starved for images, boxing, wrestling, and bodybuilding magazines became a significant pleasure.[34]

Out and outed sports stars have included the former NFL running back David Kopay, the wide receiver Jerry Smith, and the offensive tackle Roy Simmons; the Major League Baseball outfielders Glenn Burke and Billy Bean; the Olympic gold-medal swimmer Bruce Hayes; the English soccer striker Justin Fashanu; the diver Greg Louganis; the Australian rugby league forward Ian Roberts (see Chapter Two); the bodybuilding world champion Bob Jackson-Paris; the golfer Muffin Spencer-Devlin; the long-distance swimmer Diane Nyad; the skaters Matthew Hall, Rudy Galindo, and Doug Mattis; the National Hockey League referee Brett Parson; the bike racer Missy Giove; the tennis pros Gigi Fernandez and Amélie Mauresmo (see Chapter Four); the Olympic decathlete Tom Waddell; the baseball umpire Dave Pallone; the extreme athlete Rodger McFarlane; and the boxer Gina "Boom Boom" Guidi.

The names are few. Intense but denied connections between sex and sports make the terrain risky, as per horrific statistics and narratives of anti-gay sports violence, especially in U.S. colleges and high schools. Consider the blend of support and hysteria on the part of former teammates that accompanied Bean's revelations in Miami and then, spectacularly, on the front page of the *New York Times*. The militant evangelical New York Yankees pitcher Andy Pettitte said that "there would be a question of being comfortable" with a gay colleague on the team. When Mianne Bagger, who was once a man, won the 1999 South Australian Ladies Amateur golf title, GolfWeb, a key Internet site, raised the issue and revealed that the U.S. Women's Amateur and U.S. Women's Open Championship required entrants to be "female at birth."[35] A member of the Canadian women's hockey team coaching the triumphant Mighty Dykes at the New York Gay Games was said to have dodged Canadian cable-television crews during the event. The moral panic about girls being made into lesbians through sports extends beyond education and into allegations of compulsory homosexuality. A major story from the Sydney Olympics concerned Camilla Anderson from Denmark and Mia Hundvin from Norway, two women who were married to each other and competing on opposite teams in handball, despite the fact that the Danish Olympic Committee had sought to suppress media knowledge of their relationship.[36] In 1993, the cricketer Denise Annetts complained to the New South Wales Anti-Discrimination Board that she had been dropped from the Australian national side for being straight. *Sports Illustrated* set in train another moral panic with its notorious 1999 cover story "Who's Coaching Your Kid," which detailed sexual activity between male coaches and junior male athletes. Although the article acknowledged that experts did not see this as a "homosexual phenomenon," given the huge amount of sexual abuse from fathers and brothers suffered by daughters and sisters, the point was pretty much buried within a spectacular focus on non-consensual sexual practices.[37]

But there are signs of change—even in bastions of sameness. The professional women's basketball team the New York Liberty advises in its 1999 media guide that General Manager Carol Blazejowski lives with a woman and their children, while Guidi is prominently out in national boxing.[38] The Baltimore Orioles outfielder Brady Anderson's Web site has a poster shot of him that emphasizes his crotch and chest and has gained record numbers of gay adherents, about which he registers a "no comment."[39] The English film *Get Real* (1999) is a coming-of-age boyhood story in which a wimpy gay youth discovers that his toilet boyfriend is the school's ultra-jock. Combining queer politics with the prosaic life of international law can expand cultural rights, as the International Gay Rodeo Association has done over the past twenty years through its mixture of conventional competition with heterodox dress and conduct. The 1994 Gay Games even challenged its own norms. When Stephane Vachon announced his withdrawal from an ice-skating event because his partner had fallen ill, officials asked whether anyone in the crowd knew the necessary dance pattern. Charles Sinek, a straight coach, borrowed skates and took the "lady's part"—which he had long taught—and they won. That Hollywood-style trope was repeated, again with signs made to resignify, when Bill Wasmer danced as Gene Kelly to "Singin' in the Rain," shifting gears to accompany "It's Raining Men."[40]

The heart of Sportsex—the questions of what is a man, what is a woman, what they are entitled to, and how they handle their object choices—-has seen massive changes. In summary, cautious reconceptualizations of the relationship between modern biology and social science, and re-examinations of corporeality and consumption, make it apparent that bodies are now an integral concept in social theory. As John Loy et al. note: "The sporting body is a key site for studying the dynamic relationship between power, knowledge, and corporeal existence."[41] This link to social norms is equally powerful at the site of collective bodies—the nation.

Nation

Sports are a crucible of nation. Consider connections between the training of soldiers and athletes, or the strategies of generals and coaches. Carl von Clausewitz described a trinitarian form to war and the state—material enmity, physical presence, and political leadership—all of which translate to sports at both the ideological and policy levels. In each venture, victory is conceived as a purifying rite. Pierre de Coubertin founded the modern Olympics to follow the example of British muscular Christianity and redeem

French masculinity after the shocks of the Franco-Prussian War. The Mexican Revolution moved quickly to institutionalize sports in the 1910s as a sign and source of national unity. When the Argentine Olympic Committee was founded in 1922, it promised to work for "the perfection of the race and the glory of conquering what is noble, worthy, and beautiful." John F. Kennedy established the President's Council on Youth Fitness to counter a "growing softness, our increasing lack of physical fitness," which, he said, constituted "a threat to our security." From a very different angle, the Sandinistas in Nicaragua abolished professional sports, focusing instead on nation-building through a large-scale sports-for-all policy.[42]

Non-military benefits also accrue to the state from these policies. A healthier, fitter population reduces the cost of public health, guarantees a functioning workforce, and helps tourism. A recent Aotearoa/New Zealand minister of recreation and sport referred to his portfolio as a route to "social and economic prosperity" through the promotion of "active, physical lifestyles." He identified an additional benefit: "Being into sport" ensured being "out of court." This longstanding criminological obsession deems familially based and formal sporting activities to be worthy, integrative norms, while informal leisure is demonized. Even Michael Manley, the former Socialist prime minister of Jamaica (and a distinguished historian of cricket), pushed such a line: Men's violence is a danger that can be pacified and redirected into an appropriate sphere—literally, national fitness. Just as schools have often used the gymnasium for discipline, so can the nation. Come on down, Matthew Arnold. But more than that, sports become inflected with an ethnocentric notion of correct behavior that associates delinquency with racial minorities and youthful muscularity. Given diminished employment prospects in the latter half of the twentieth century, such moral panic has as much to do with governments' preparing people for a leisure-defined poverty as with their training them to work (see Chapter Three).[43]

The heavily symbolic components to this association inexorably return such policies to chauvinistic national mythmaking. The U.S. Peace Corps argued in *Sports Illustrated* in 1963 that sports were more productive terrain for its mission than teaching because they were less "vulnerable to charges of 'neo-colonialism' and 'cultural imperialism.'" Perhaps, but sports can be serious business. The 1969 Central American Soccer war broke out when the Honduran government expelled all Salvadorans following a match between the two countries. The events of 1989 in Central and Eastern Europe were characterized by intense passions associated with sports. Steaua team military athletes shot at the secret police in Romania; Dinamo Club players defended their patrons, the Securitate (secret police), and the captain of the national rugby union side died in battle. In East Germany, the figure skater Katharina Witt and the swimmers Roland Matthes and Kornelia Ender had their homes sacked. That reaction repeats the treatment of Astylus when he switched nationalities prior to the Olympics in 480 B.C.: His old house was destroyed.[44]

Sporting allegory has traditionally reinforced masculinism and patriotism, especially at times of great conflict and formal celebration. U.S. Secretary of Defense Melvin Laird euphemized the mining of Haiphong Harbor and increased bombing of North Vietnam as "an expansion ball club"; the Nixon White House staff called itself "Operation Linebacker," and Tricky Dicky's own nickname was "quarterback." Promotions for Australia's 1991 rugby league series between New South Wales and Queensland referred to the players as "scuds" and "patriots." During his presidency, the oleaginous Ronald Reagan regularly cited the role he played as footballer George Gipp in *Knute Rockne, All American*, the 1940 biopic of a Notre Dame football coach. This was supposed to stand as a universal sign of Americanness. Reagan quoted Gipp's dying words that had inspired the side to new heights—"Win one for the Gipper"—in his 1981 commencement address at the university commemorated in the film, when opening the 1984 Los Angeles

Olympics, as a rallying cry during the Nevada Senate race in 1986, and at George Bush's nomination two years later. He also trivialized his 1984 presidential opponent Walter Mondale as "Coach Tax Hike."[45] Such metaphorizations associate romantic male sacrifice with national glory through classic second-order meaning. The Gipp exemplar takes the mythic last words of a historical character as replayed in a film. Four decades later, the actor playing him redeploys the words for political purposes, cleaving to himself the persona of the original speaker. Enunciation loses historical specificity, and banality benefits. Thought disorder reigns.

Such stereotypes function as ethical norms that generate new habits amongst the citizenry. Still, fissures do appear. In their analysis of Australian nationalism and the Olympics, David Rowe and Geoffrey Lawrence note that the media "break out into a nationalistic sweat" when a new star emerges. The appearance of such a star is an opportunity for the "unbounded rather than qualified exultation" that accompanies winning an ultimate prize. It calls up Horatio Algerish myths about a meritocracy in which all can rise to their deserved level of achievement and reward. The "hero or heroine embodies an abstraction ... [the spirit of the nation] and so helps to heal concrete rifts ... between competing social groups."[46] The sports star is simultaneously a product of popular culture, a marketing system, a social sign, a national emblem, the outcome of capitalism and individualism, and an object of both personal and public consumption. What Christine Gledhill has said of film stars is true on the track: They "personalise social meanings and ideologies." A person becomes a star when her off-track lifestyle and personality merge their function and significance with her sporting achievements. Performances become an amalgam of training, playing, and the self. Their bodies may be caked in mud or clad in uniforms, but their names, numbers, sponsors, case histories, and smiles can all be retrieved and replayed by the electronic brush of history. These signs provide the mechanics of what ethnomethodologists refer to as the "personalized stranger," a figure known through media intimacy rather than direct human interaction.[47]

Stardom imbricates the private and the public, the non-performative and the performative, the intimate and the public, and it offers appropriation by marginal groups (gay women and Martina Navratilova; African American youth and Michael Jordan). The intertextuality of the private and the public blurs the private agency of personal characteristics with the public domain of socially meaningful activity. This is particularly complex, because stars stand in ambivalent relation to capital and labor. Stars may, for instance, set up companies that profit "from the sale of their own personae."[48] If stars fail to appear, fall from grace, or are in some way compromised, social cleavages emerge anew.

That encourages us to interrogate who stands for the nation in gender and racial terms. Consider efforts by U.S. colleges to recruit athletes who can heighten a school's institutional standing as a nationally prominent entity that does more (or perhaps less) than educate. The "latter-day scramble for Africa" was an unseemly search for African track-and-field stars from that began in the 1970s. It resembled nineteenth-century imperial powers seeking new territory. In 1960, U.S. colleges recruited 8 percent of their athletes from Africa. By 1980, the figure had rise to 33 percent, following numerous Olympic successes by middle-distance runners. Once African student-athletes came to the United States, they were brutally overworked to service boosterism, returning home with devastated bodies that allowed no room for further success on behalf of their own countries. Approximately 75 percent of local and international black male athletes on U.S. sports scholarships do not gain degrees, and many NCAA schools never graduate freshman-class sports scholars. Nor do sports lead to personal success for the students. Black men and women are much more likely to become doctors, lawyers, and dentists than professional athletes. For all men and women, the prospects for upward mobility from sports vary between 0.004 percent and

0.007 percent, and there appears to be a shorter career span for African American professional baseball players than for white players, who are kept on longer after their prime.[49]

Women of color occupy a particularly ambiguous position in American sports. Although the Olympic triumphs of African American female sprinters since the 1960s have given them (quadrennial) national attention, they have suffered sexist and racist depictions in the media. For when women are given the mantle of national sporting symbolism, it is always overdetermined. Consider the 1996 Olympic gymnasts, hailed by the media as "The Face of America." What did this mean? They supposedly formed "The Face" because of diversity: the team included one Asian American (Amy Chow) and an African American (Dominique Dawes) amid white representatives. In two previous Olympics, Dawes had been joined by another black gymnast, Betty Okino. In 1992 and 1996, publicists had not talked that team up in the same way. Blackness did not constitute promotable diversity.[50]

And this issue extends well beyond the United States. In 1990, the *Los Angeles Times* published what became an infamous interview with the British Tory politician Norman Tebbitt, who charged migration with endangering the "special relationship" between the United Kingdom and the United States. He also suggested that Britain impose a "cricket test" on migrants: Asking "Which side do they cheer for?" would sort out whether South Asians in England watching the local side play Pakistan or India had adequately assimilated. In the House of Commons itself, Tebbitt related this question to death threats against Salman Rushdie before warming to his real intention: keeping Hong Kong Chinese (British subjects) from migrating before the handover to China in 1997.[51] When South Asians flew into London's Heathrow Airport for the 1999 World Cup of cricket, officials reportedly gave them a "cricket quiz" to decide whether their level of knowledge meant they were really there to watch. South Africans were not subjected to this test (perhaps it was assumed they were "white").

After Hassiba Boulmerka won the women's 1,500 meters at the 1991 World Athletic Championships, she was feted by President Chadli Benjedid on return to Algeria. Boulmerka was denounced by segments of Islam, however, for displaying her legs on television, and subsequently moved to France, winning Olympic gold the next year in Barcelona under the pall of death threats.[52] During the mid-summer 1994 World Cup of Soccer, Iranian TV viewers were reportedly shown a special montage: Whenever U.S. cameras cut to shots of the crowd, programmers in Iran offered footage of people in winter garb from other matches, hiding decadent Western attire from their fragile audience. Meanwhile, U.S. marketers continued to advertise the sport as more truly international than the World Series and the Super Bowl, which look pitifully intramural to outsiders. A problem at one site—difference and diaspora—is a virtue at another, with the media a defining site.

Media

The bowler's Holding the batsman's Willey. —*Cricket commentary, BBC (1976)*

Textualization has long been a feature of Sportsex. Homoerotic sporting texts, for instance, have a long lineage—the late-nineteenth-century popular novel *Raffles*, to give one example. In *Raffles*, the story of a ruling-class British cricketer and jewel thief is told by a male narrator through thinly coded admiration:

> Again I see him, leaning back in one of the luxurious chairs with which his room was furnished. I see his indolent, athletic figure; his pale, sharp, clean-shaven features; his curly black hair; his strong, unscrupulous mouth. And again I feel the clear beam of his wonderful eye, cold and luminous as a star, shining into my brain—sifting the very secrets of my heart.[53]

The male body is sports' everyday currency and is up for mockery as much as fandom. As Ann says of Farley Granger in Alfred Hitchcock's *Strangers on a Train* (1951), "He looks so silly in his tennis clothes." This currency is most unusual in societies where "man" stands for everyone and is rarely subject to specific inquiry other than through feminisms. Paul Smith points out that when masculinity is "understood simply as a given," there is little room for transforming it. But once it is identified as partial and contingent, its "state of silent and indefinite normality over and against which difference was both established and measured" is made audible, definite, and itself subject to difference.[54] The sense of sports as a site of struggle over contemporary definitions of masculinity is not recent. In 1869, the Cincinnati Red Stockings baseball team's song referenced the female gaze:

> We are a band of baseball players
> From Cincinnati City;
> We come to toss the ball around
> And sing to you our ditty;
> ... The ladies want to know
> Who are those gallant men in
> Stockings red, they'd like to know.[55]

And consider these stories from the archive of Mass-Observation, that strange blend of British surrealism and empiricism that saw a vast array of data gathered about ordinary life in the late 1930s and early 1940s:

> Wrestling at first disgusted me, but now I like it very much. No other sport has such fine husky specimens of manhood as wrestling. I find it such a change to see real he men after the spineless and insipid men one meets ordinarily. —*"A woman,"* *1938*

> I love it because it brings back to me, I am 67 years of age, my young days when men were men and not the namby pamby, simpering, artificial, hair curling variety that is most prevalent in the present day generation. —*"A man," 1938*[56]

It's pretty clear that concerns were being voiced by women and older men about the quality of maleness on offer—this at a moment of national crisis. Today, the requirement for capitalism to generate new forms of consumption has driven masculinity and heteronormativity into a condition of unparalleled flux, as capital targets hitherto unwanted sports consumers: queers and straight women. I believe that just such differentiation has taken Sport-sex to a new sphere. So as sports move away from violence and toward inclusive audience strategies, the boxer is supplanted by (or becomes) the centerfold. The progressive displacement of speech by sight as a critical hermeneutic method, which began in early-modern Europe, at last moves onto men in the sexual way that colonized women much earlier.

But this shift away from a heroization of male achievement that conventionally excluded women is recent: Media sports have been staggeringly masculinist. Most nations dedicate less than 5 percent of press coverage to female athletes, and what there is frequently condescends and trivializes.[57] In 1989, women's sports received 5 percent of sporting coverage on national U.S. sports cable TV and Los Angeles television stations. In 1999, the figure was 8.7 percent.[58] Messner et al.'s study of American basketball and tennis reveals that commentators have marked female athletes and women's sports by infantilizing these women as individuals and framing their achievements ambivalently. Jim McKay and Debbie Huber have demonstrated how specific "technologies/techniques of gender" anchor images of men's and women's bodies in ways that naturalize the sporting superiority of men while marginalizing and incorporating women. Similarly, Laurie Schulze has argued that representations of female bodybuilders are implicated in a "recuperative strategy" to reposition women within permissible spaces. So *Time* magazine's 1982 cover story "Coming on Strong, The New Ideal of Beauty" endorsed athletic femininity because "men may decide it is sexy for one basic reason: it can enhance sex."[59]

In her analysis of Olympic Games photography, Margaret Carlisle Duncan argues that women are represented as subordinate and sexually inviting and men as dominant. Content analyses of

Sports Illustrated demonstrate misogynistic and white biases. For example, in 1993 the magazine's 52 covers featured six women: a tennis player with a knife in her neck, a swimsuit model, the widows of two baseball players, the victim of assaults by a father, and the victim of an assault paid for by a rival.[60] That year, the magazine's list of the forty people who were deemed to have contributed the most to sports included just four women. *Sports Illustrated* has recently re-emphasized its status as a bastion of late masculinism, with female reporters and readers encouraged to go elsewhere.[61] And in 1999, the magazine was pleased to run advertisements such as Jim Beam's proud claim (accompanied by a graphic of young men drinking in a bar) that "Unlike Your Girlfriend, They [fellow men or glasses of bourbon—take your pick] Never Ask Where This Relationship Is Going" (1 November 1999). The most widely read segment of newspapers, the sports pages, routinely give greater attention to animals than women. And women's sports and fitness magazines allot the vast majority of their attention to white women.[62] In Britain, a raft of "New Lad" magazines emerged across the 1990s, emphasizing alcohol, sex, anti-feminism, sport spectatorship, and anti-fitness.[63] The depiction of women in *Sports Illustrated*'s swimsuit issue continues to trouble feminists, their supporters, and some sports "purists" (the latter for their own reasons).[64] This annual issue of soft-core poses has as much to do with women and sports as *Baywatch* has to do with lifesaving—in fact, next time you're grasping for a way to illustrate the idea of a structural homology. . . .

There are signs of counter-power. The 1990s saw the emergence of Womensport Australia, a sports subsection to the Australian Federation of Business and Professional Women, which analyzed the women's share of 1988 summer Olympic coverage, and of the Women's Electoral Lobby Sport Action Group. In addition to criticizing televised sports as occupied terrain, many contemporary feminists claim sportswomen as key components of the national sporting imaginary.[65] The latter-day appearance of "other" categories of viewer as objects of desire for advertisers makes the televisual gaze on the male sporting body more and more sexualized and polysemic. Attacking this shift from action to spectacle, as per Lasch's critique outlined earlier, fits with the logic of gendered assaults on popular culture, which associate its assumed passivity with the feminization that accompanies any shift from "doing" to "consuming." Consumer capitalism's emphasis on constructing desire is said to embody a loss of masculine productiveness in favor of feminine circularity: Mining and manufacturing are supplanted as economic staples by the emotional labor of the service industries. A sporting example can be found in the once-conventional derogation by men of women's tennis by way of direct and unfavorable comparisons between sudden, heaving force and subtle, mounting strategems. Male players sometimes claim that they are "better" in direct competition than the best women, so women should receive less prize money, regardless of spectator interest or alternative weightings of skill. When these antinomies break down, there is consternation (see Chapter Four). The irony is that Lasch-like purists often prefer women's team sports to men's, because the former are thought to embody traditional virtues of teamwork, humility, and historical awe toward earlier stars.[66] Content analysis of U.S. consumer magazines demonstrates this point vividly. A comparison of images of men in such magazines in 1964, 1983, and 1993 reveals the rapid sexualization of the male form across the 1990s. In the decade to 1993, women were three times more likely to be portrayed in a sexualized manner, but explicit and suggestively alluring representations of men had become much more common—up from 11 percent to 18 percent of images. Male pin-ups are common today in teen magazines and British tabloid newspapers. Content analysis of press coverage of the Atlanta Olympics shows changes afoot in the U.S. media. Five key newspapers dedicated disproportionately high amounts of coverage to female athletes: They commented more on men's appearance than women's, were more critical of men's foibles and blemishes, and mentioned men's family arrangements more often than women's. The notion of contradictions between work and family characterized references to women more than men, but this may have to do with sexist social relations rather than media tropes.

The burden of Sportsex is that this sexualization has become a roundabout, not a one-way, street. Commercial sports today are a site for activating the female gaze and even empowering it, part of a momentum that is putting the public presentation of men under scrutiny in the same way as women. Men, too, are becoming dependent on the gaze directed at them. Sports have always licensed men to watch and dissect other men's bodies in fetishistic detail, a legitimate space for men to gaze on the male form. The male caress is generally accepted by media commentators, because it is associated with friendship and struggle; it is almost part of the game. Paradoxically, the fact that such contact is so openly looked at renders it acceptable. So sports are both a regulatory space for investigating the foibles of men and a privileged space of the legitimate gaze of male upon male. But TV performance and public analysis of the phenomenon can be unsettling, as when a magistrate in Alice Springs, Australia, sentenced a man for indecent exposure in 1989, commenting that there was a clear link between his conduct and the Australian cricket team's "homosexual-type behaviour" and "unmanly activities" (embracing one another after a successful play).[67]

For straight female viewers, immense sexual pleasure can come from watching men's bodies at play on television, albeit away from narrational and statistical fetishes: "Here were barely clad, eyeable Aussie male bodies in top anatomical nick. The cameras follow their rough and tumble disport with a relentless precision, in wide-angle, close-up and slow-motion replay. With the commentary turned down and with some music the imagery may be released from its imposed fixity of meaning and the performance enjoyed as choreographed spectacle: lyrical, flagrantly masculine, and erotic."[68]

Who is the implied spectator of TV sports? In early 1990s
Canada, the beer company that owned the sports cable network
TSN sought an isomorphism of sporting content, audience, and
beer intake by living up to its advertising motto: "We deliver the
male." As late as 1998, an advertisement for ESPN in *Broadcasting and Cable* magazine promised "More tackles, less tutus."[69] But
commercial and cultural changes are exerting tremendous pressure on the normativity of sports, endangering the seemingly rock-
solid maleness at its core. Far from seeing sports—especially on
TV—as unacceptable and unwanted, U.S. female spectators tune
in to the Olympics in large numbers. The 1992 Winter Games
drew 57 percent of its U.S. TV audience from women. Women's
figure skating drew higher ratings than that year's World Series
and the NCAA basketball championship game. And the women's
technical skating program at the 1994 Winter Games drew the
fourth-highest ratings of any program in U.S. history, right alongside the final episode of *M*A*S*H*. In 1995, more women than
men in Britain watched Wimbledon tennis on television, and the
numbers were nearly equal for boxing. In the 1998 NBA playoffs,
more women were drawn to game seven of the Bulls–Pacers series
than to the situation comedy *Veronica's Closet* or the drama series
ER. That year, the women's final at the U.S. Open out-rated the
men's by 15 percent. Every major professional men's league in the
United States now has a women's media marketing plan. Meanwhile, male spectatorship of TV sport in the United States is in
serious decline, as more and more viewers turn to the History and
Discovery channels. The perennial savior of network sportscast-
ers, the NFL, saw the ratings for *Monday Night Football* at record
lows in 1998–99 and 1999–2000 over its thirty years in existence,
while a third of its audience was female. In 1999, more men aged
18–34 viewed professional women's softball on ESPN2 than
watched arena football, the National Hockey League, or Major
League Soccer.[70] Something is happening. A clue comes from
ABC's coverage of Super Bowl 2000, which showed the Giants

cornerback Jason Seahorn in uniform pants during a pregame show—about which Meredith Vieira offered that football is "all about the butt."[71]

This demography prompts particular genres of presentation. U.S. TV executives operate from the assumption that women are attracted to biographical and conceptual narratives about stars and their sports rather than to statistics and quests for success. So NBC initiated a "female-inclusive sports subgenre" at the 1992 Summer Games, offering "private-life" histories of selected contestants. NBC targeted women and families in 1996 to such effect that 50 percent of its Olympic audience consisted of adult women and 35 percent men, with women's gymnastics one of the most popular events and men's boxing and wrestling edged out of prime time (although a disproportionate address in general of men's versus women's sport remained on screen). The network reported an increase of 26 percent in the number of female viewers aged 25 to 54 by comparison with the 1992 Barcelona Games.

Of course, this welcome shift is part of a wholesale, commodifying impact of capital and TV on sports. But we must acknowledge developments that are relatively autonomous from the logics and processes of business.[72] For instance, the careful development of character produced for the English soccer player Paul Gascoigne during BBC and ITV coverage of the 1990 World Cup of Soccer began with the spoiled and underdone Wunderkind, unaware of his own abilities and prone to inane acts of juvenilia. A series of profiles culminated in an emotional interview, which then became an object of analysis for the watching panel of experts. The interviewee's performance drew special praise from another international player, touched by "hearing his voice quiver."[73] This tremulous oscillation between the hot and sweaty and the removed and clinical is characteristic of both commentary and sports masculinity. The dual constitution of Gascoigne as tough and soft, by turns impossibly arrogant and impossibly tender, suggests that the activity we are witnessing is far more complicated than any account of TV sports as beholden to masculine hegemony or capitalist rationality will allow. For when Jimmy Hill observes that "the danger with the developing countries [is] that they can't defend their own goal area against high crosses," or John Helm reacts to a shot of a T-shirt covered with the autographs of the Cameroon team by saying, "Well, they can all sign their names," we are not so much in the domain of Eurocentric domination as thought disorder, recognizable and mockable as such. And the fact that Bruce McAvaney of Australia's Channel 10 exclaimed from the Olympic pool in 1988, "Medals for Suriname and Costa Rica, what is the world coming to?" could just as easily turn our minds to questions of globalized culture as encourage us to follow his ethnocentrism. After all, this is the man who back-announced the 100 meters at the 1987 world track-and-field title event with: "Carl Lewis. I love him."[74]

Training in commentary extends to methods for emphasizing the personal, gladiatorial aspect of sports, further sexualizing them. In place of the thick description offered by radio, the thinness of TV commentary produces narratives of individuation that seek out difference, character, history, and conflict as momentary distractions from the excitement or boredom of the main play. Heroic qualities are logocentrically dependent on low, base, undesirable, and, above all, different (non-heroic) behavior. Investing sports with drama as an embellishment is therefore integral to commentary.[75] Instructions to broadcasters such as the following are not uncommon: "Create a feeling that the competitors don't like each other. . . . Studies have shown that fans react better, and are more emotionally involved, if aggressive hostility is present. . . . Work the audience at the emotional level and get them involved in the game."[76]

The tight interplay of technology and emotion is clear from instructions that Australia's Channel 9 used for many years to train its cricket commentators: "Think constantly of voice-over cassettes, animations, computers and anything which will help the viewer enjoy the telecast. . . . Remember this is a game of many and varied hues. As a commentator you will keep foremost in your mind that cricket contains venom and courage, drama and humour, and you will not be backward in bringing out in your commentary those aspects of the noble and ancient pastime"[77]

As a baseball TV director explains, "I'm trying to establish that tense relationship between the pitcher and the batter . . . that impression of a face-off." In Britain, television companies make it clear to athletics officials that they require "head-to-head confrontations." And when the 1983 Indianapolis 500 ran without incident, ABC's replay included a segment on safety issues, an excuse for featuring extended highlights of death and destruction from earlier, more riveting contests.[78]

Although deriding opponents is not obvious in promotions for some sports ("Seven's Summer of Tennis"), it is quite clear in interstate rugby league games (as when New South Wales teams are called "Cockroaches") and in these segments from international cricket's TV theme songs: "Each game, the stakes get higher, the white ball is on fire. . . . We'll bring him to his knees, just watch him bend," "revenge," "disgrace," "carve each other up in the World Series Cup," "gentlemen, we'll tan your flamin' hide," and "standing trial."[79] Of course, when such gladiatorial contests go the wrong way—or, worse still, don't go very far at all, in that they are dull or obvious—commentators receive further instructions: "Some games are unexciting, boring contests where one side or the other clobbers the competition. You want to keep the audience's attention for as long as possible and keep them and the sponsors happy. The best way to keep the audience is to limit giving the time and score, and concentrate on the immediate action that occurs. Take the game out of context and work on the game one play at a time."[80]

This insistence on keeping interest alive extends to re-forming various sports or imposing rules to suit TV coverage that split professional from amateur codes. The exemplar is wrestling. After great successes with female viewers in the 1940s and 1950s on French and American television, wrestling's popularity with the networks fell away, a victim of the departure from efforts to attract general audiences in favor of the male spectator and his disposable income. The United States reintroduced the sport on cable television in the 1980s, using hand-held video cameras in extreme close-ups of the action to emphasize the spectacular. Wrestling's return involves a new address of women and a revised set of rules. The notion of a quick fall, a set of tightly circumscribed moves, and rigorous refereeing have been forsaken. In their stead, we see a circuslike activity dominated by absurd persons in silly costumes, who adopt exotic personae and seek the acrobatic and the showy as a path to success.[81] The iconography plays quite spectacularly with gay and feminized images of men. In the mid-'90s, New Jersey legally defined wrestling as entertainment rather than sport, thereby removing the cost of maintaining medical facilities (a requirement at sporting events). The caring and sharing legislators of the Garden State were able to cut promoters' costs and hence attract TV-staged bouts.

Sports, then, pick up the body as an icon of difference, coloring it with commercial and cultural referents. The commodification and medicalization of the sporting body have effects that none can predict. Chapter Two traces some of these unintended consequences with specific reference to masculinity.

Commodifying the Male Body = Problematizing Hegemonic Masculinity?

As part of a gathering critique across the human sciences and social movements, we have seen a burst of writing and thinking about men across the '80 and '90s, from self-help to feminist and queer theory.[1] Most critical research into men and sport draws its inspiration from the idea that we live in an era of "hegemonic masculinity" (HM). The concept's lineage is in the writings of Antonio Gramsci, as picked up and redisposed by Robert W. Connell. For Gramsci, an Italian Marxist writing from prison in the mid-1930s, hegemony is a contest of meanings in which a ruling class gains consent to the social order by making its power appear normal and natural. Ordinary people give "'spontaneous' consent" to the "general direction imposed on social life by the dominant fundamental group" as a consequence of the education and entertainment provided by intellectuals. The society contains old cultural meanings and practices, no longer dominant but still influential, and emergent ones, either propagated by an upcoming class or incorporated by the ruling elite.

These discourses are expressed by intellectuals, who work at "superstructural 'levels'" to forge the "hegemony which the dominant group exercises throughout society."[2]

Connell, an Australian Marxist writing from Australian and U.S. research universities in the 1980s and '90s, applies this notion of consent through incorporation to gender relations, especially masculinity. Combining theories of imperialism with feminism, he articulates the history of North Atlantic commercial republics expanding into the rest of the world with contemporary anthropological study. The result makes Western European and North American white male sexuality isomorphic with power: Men seek global dominion and desire, orchestrated to oppress women. HM encompasses obvious sexism—rape, domestic violence, and obstacles to women's occupational advancement—and more subtle "tactics" of domination, such as the exclusion of women from social environments and sports teams and lopsided media interest in the lives and bodies of men. Connell calls for critical investigations of masculinity across the state, work, the family, sexual practice, and organizational life.[3]

This model seems to fit sports' ideological apparatus, where aggression, bodily force, competition, and physical skill are primarily associated with straight maleness.[4] For example, Jim McKay says, "Any male Australian athlete will verify . . . the most insulting accusation a coach can make about a players performance is to say that he 'played like a sheila' or a 'poofter.'"[5] In H. L. Schwartz's words, "being or appearing homosexual will bring shame to the team and the sport."[6] No surprise, then, that the British heavyweight boxer Lennox Lewis reacts to queries about dating with, "I'm fully 110 percent a ladies' man. You don't have to worry about me."[7] HM's homophobia and misogyny are personified by the infamous former Indiana University basketball coach Bobby Knight. Consider this hysterical 1985 assault on one player: "You never push yourself. You know what you are, Daryl? You are the worst fucking pussy I've ever seen play basketball at

this school. The absolute worst pussy ever. You have more god-
damn ability than 95 percent of the players we've had here, but
you are a pussy from the top of your head to the bottom of your
feet. An absolute fucking pussy."[8]

Of course, HM (straight, strong, domineering) oppresses the
many men excluded from it, while even "subscribers" may find
its norms unattainable. HM's articulation against women and
homosexuals makes it unpopular with vast numbers of people.
Although men who feel socially weak (the working class, minorities, and many immigrants) may find the hegemonic model
appealing, the real sources of their powerlessness lie in the mon-
etary and racial economy, not in struggles against women and
gays.[9] Connell himself argues that male identity is complex and
polyvalent, with no singular set of qualities consistently marked
as masculine. Masculinity and men's bodies (symbolically conceived as unitary) are contested sites, fraught with contradictions.[10] In an in-depth interview with an Australian sporting professional who seemingly embodies HM, Connell's subject is asked
about the meaning of being a man. He replies in negative terms:
To be a man is to "not be a gay." The exclusion of male desire
for other men from the definition of masculinity occurs in the
context of all-male competition and single-sex affinity on and off
the sporting field. Connell observes a profound contradiction in
this "articulation of self and body." The body is invested with nar-
cissistic social currency as an object for professional improvement
and success, but this narcissism is unstable and can never be sat-
isfied. The commodified body requires constant self-surveillance
and renewal if it is to remain competitive and, hence, marketable
to sponsors.

Connell's social theory is impressive, notably in its attention to
history. But critics point to the fact that the histories he sketches
tend to be brief and conveniently selected, such that the work
sometimes reads like neat ideal types overlying messy evidence.
Counter-examples to a narrative of Western domination abound

in the Third World, and there are significant aspects of everyday men's conduct that are about selflessness and the desire to build, not to rule or destroy.[11] Wil Coleman, by contrast, calls for a focus on masculinity in use—not as a term freighted-in from ideal types, as per Connell, but when maleness appears as such in the vocabulary of everyday life.[12] Football is one example, because it repeatedly elaborates what is "manly," associated as it is with "guys in huddles, accepting orders."[13]

The thing about hegemony as a concept is that it explains everything and nothing in a circular motion. Tending to lack a dynamic of history made at specific sites, it accounts for seemingly resistive moves to domination as a function of repressive tolerance, or as co-opted by ruling logics. Such moves are rarely investigated for themselves but as symptoms of politics from elsewhere, and this "elsewhere" is the given of whoever currently rules. Aspects of everyday conduct or reading that are inconsistent with standard political or textual moves are understood in the same way. But perhaps they have nothing to do with consent to domination elsewhere. Perhaps they are site-specific or articulated through dynamics other than HM. Does HM allow for a time when men are not being men, when their activities might be understood as discontinuous, conflicted, and ordinary rather than interconnected, functional, and dominant—when nothing they do relates to the overall subordination of women or their own self-formation as a gendered group?

Using HM-style formulations, many gender-studies sociolinguists claim that stereotypes subjugate women. This is undoubtedly true. But while some stereotypes can be removed or discredited through critique, genres of speech that categorize people are ineradicable. Harvey Sacks argues that stereotypes (he calls them "categorials") are vital techniques in the culture of everyday life. Everybody generalizes about "we" and "they." These are routine cultural devices for explaining both mundane and unusual intersubjective events.[14] I do not suggest that all categorials are equally desirable or that they cannot be policed in the interests of a more democratically accountable world of meaning. Rather, I doubt that language exists without them.[15]

Much queer theory and postcolonial writing—sensibly, in my view—seeks to rearticulate existing categorials, not destroy them. To use Hannah Arendt's maxim: "One can resist only in terms of the identity that is under attack." Taken a step further, this is D. A. Miller's plea for gay creativity to avoid the boredom and orthodoxy of "positive images" and Stuart Hall calling for "a piece of [the] action" that once stereotyped blackness: not denying or replacing existing images, but rearticulating what is, in any case, always already internalized and dispersed. This has been around as an argument within feminism for twenty years, at least since the journal *m/f* pointed out the impossibility of identifying accurate generic images of women that might displace categorials.[16]

Most critical theorists opposed to the HM model look for alternatives in the psychological interiority of men. Brian Pronger claims that the very basis of sports is "a covert world of homoeroticism." He does not suggest that all sportsmen are gay; rather, he argues that segregation in sports by gender requires sportsmen to form their most intimate bonds with the same sex.[17] Elisabeth Badinter explains this trend as a function of the "requirement" that masculinity differentiate itself from women. Men's lives come from the bodies of women, from whom they must disentangle their identities. This struggle produces numerous effects, such as that women are less emotionally disturbed during adolescence and live longer, and men resent women while also questioning the role of their fathers.[18] Badinter draws on the Oedipus myth, which concerns a man whose feet are brutally bound and disfigured during childhood by his father and who later unwittingly carries out a prediction that he will kill his father and marry his mother. On discovering the fact, Oedipus tears his eyes out. This story helps to explain the transfer of boys' affection from mothers to other women and accounts for succession and rivalry in male life. It takes violence as the narrative touchstone of masculinity.[19] The literary-theological anthropologist René Girard also focuses on violence. He suggests that there is a tripartite and mimetic character to men's desire, "not only a subject and an object but a third presence as well: the rival." Both the subject and the rival want the object. This is not due to its innate properties. Rather, the rival's desire "alerts the subject to the desirability of the object." Girard identifies sacrificial violence as the key to holding together social formations that lack a fully achieved juridical apparatus. A subject is selected onto whom the tensions of a group can be projected. Sometimes this subject is an enemy (a soccer player from another club) and sometimes it is a friend (casual violence among the team at practice or socially). This sacrificial figure is a surrogate.[20] Such an argument sees violence as a problem of social order, not of HM.

However we differ, most analysts agree that the crucial issue in discussing men is power—that everywhere one turns, men seem to be in power, but everywhere one listens, they seem to feel powerless.[21] I want to suggest, contra Connell, that this feeling is a partially positive byproduct of the commodification of male beauty; and contra Badinter and Girard, that it is historically contingent and political rather than timelessly universal and psychological.

Selling Boyhood

[Terry] Bradshaw began saying of [Mike] Webster, "I loved him from the very first moment I put my hands under his butt," and he followed with an anecdote about how Iron Mike liked to drink a gallon of buttermilk and take liver pills before games, which meant that by the fourth quarter he was ripping eye-watering farts as Bradshaw squatted over him. . . . At the end of his speech, Bradshaw produced a football and hollered, "Jes' one more time!" Webster took off his gold jacket and squatted, and . . . [Bradshaw] got up under his butt for old times' sake. —Jeremy Seabrook (1997, 51)

The commodification of sports stars across the 1990s has destabilized the HM thesis.[22] This commodification has been so dramatic that it may also invalidate generalized psychological accounts of male identity. The professionalization of sports for sponsorship purposes, a loosening of working-class masculinist domination, the appearance of women as broadcasters and journalists in the area, feminist sports scholarship, the "pink dollar" market among gay and lesbian consumers, increasing desires on the part of cable and satellite TV to broaden coverage as traditional sports are purchased by the networks, the growth of live and archival Webcasts, and political inquiries into biases against women's sports in the media all problematize the old shibboleths about men's domination of sports.

In addition to this, the very homosocial world of men's sports touches on the erotic—"the paradoxical play of masculinity" whereby "a satisfying sports competition is much the same as a satisfying homosexual, that is paradoxical, fuck." It amounts to a meeting of coeval power displaced from the site of the overtly carnal. The contestants are "accomplices" in a bizarre combination of struggle and cooperation via intensely rule-governed practices.[23] None of this is to argue for a model of repression in which an innate homosexuality in all men is finally allowed free play. But the prevalence of cross-dressing by Anglo-Celtic soccer players (think of Australia's *Footy Show* on Channel 9 or endless rugby-club tours) may be signs of same-sex desire that frequently accompany not only its disavowal but also physical assaults on gay men. What is going on when the *Footy Show* has a "Pick Your Bum" contest in which four players, attired in nothing but G-strings, poke their bottoms through holes in a divider on the set while women on-camera guess the anus that belongs to each participant?[24]

Less ambiguously, in the mid-'80s, the Sydney Swans Australian Rules club self-consciously marketed itself to the gay community, hiring a public-relations firm that designed form-hugging shorts for the club's full-forward Warwick Capper.[25] Capper came to be known on the radio network JJJ-FM as "Captain Cucumber." Even though many journalists made fun of his masculinity, gay-male and straight-female audiences appreciated just that.

This was part of emergent advertising trends. The 1980s saw two crucial conferences that helped shift the direction of global advertising: "Reclassifying People" and "Classifying People." Traditional ways to understand consumers—race and class—were supplanted by categories of self-display, with market researchers dubbing the '90s the decade of the "new man." Lifestyle and psychographic research became central issues in targeting consumers, who were divided among "moralists," "trendies," "the indifferent," "working-class puritans," "sociable spenders," and "pleasure seekers," with men further subdivided into "pontificators," "self-admirers," "self-exploiters," "token triers," "chameleons," "avant-gardicians," "sleepwalkers," and "passive endurers."[26] These innovative classifications were harbingers of new male targets for capitalist consumption.

Gay magazines circulate information to businesses about the spending power of their putatively childless, middle-class readership. *Campaign* magazine's slogan in advertising circles is "Gay Money, Big Market; Gay Market, Big Money." The 1990s brought U.S. TV commercials showing two men furnishing their apartment together at Ikea and a car-buying male couple at Toyota; at the same time, Hyundai began appointing gay-friendly staff to dealerships, IBM targeted gay-run small businesses, Subaru advertisements on buses and billboards had gay-advocacy bumper stickers and registration plates coded to appeal to queers, and Volkswagen commercials featured two men driving around in search of home furnishings. (These campaigns are known as "encrypted ads" or "gay vague." They are designed to make queers feel special for being "in the know" while not offending straights who are unable to read the codes.) Polygram's classical-music division has a special gay-promotions budget; Miller beer was a major supporter of Gay Games '94; Bud Light sponsored the 1999 San Francisco Folsom Street Fair, "the world's largest leather event"; and Coors introduced domestic-partner employee benefits to counteract its anti-gay image of the past (the offering of such benefits was echoed by the major auto manufacturers in 2000). In the late '90s, Sony, Smirnoff, and Telstra sponsored Syd-

ney's Gay and Lesbian Mardi Gras Festival. The spring 1997 U.S.
TV season saw twenty-two queer characters across the prime-
time network schedule—clear signs of niche targeting. A 2000
magazine advertisement for Mitchell Gold furniture featured a little girl sitting between two women—she might have been their
sister or their adopted child. The same year, two male characters
kissed on the TV program *Dawson's Creek*.[27] And 1999 brought
the first successful gay initial public offering—an Australian newspaper and real-estate firm—and gay and lesbian Web sites were
drawing significant private investment. Bruce Hayes, an "out"
gay man who won a gold medal for the United States in the swimming relays at the 1984 Olympics in Los Angeles, was a key figure in Levi Strauss's 1998–99 Dockers campaign. The next year,
Procter & Gamble, the nation's second-largest advertiser, dropped
plans to advertise on a TV talk show to be hosted by the anti-
queer advice-giver Laura Schlessinger following lobbying
efforts.[28] And lest we think this is an entirely Western phenomenon, the movie *Satree Lex* might have us think again. Released in
March 2000, it quickly became the second-highest-grossing Thai
film worldwide. It is based on a real volleyball team, almost
entirely made up of cross-dressing men, who won the national
amateur title in 1996.

This commodification has distinct limits, however. *Playboy* magazine featured the "vivacious and curvaceous" figure skater Katarina Witt in a December 1998 nude pictorial, part of her successful sale of sexuality. Her gay colleagues, by contrast, have to hide
their sexuality if they are to secure endorsements.[29] Of course, this
is not to suggest that Witt's actual sex life or sense of self are characterized by an appearance in *Playboy*. Rather, it points to a double standard in representational politics.

It would be naïve to see these changes as a reversal of roles
between men and women or as the triumph of polymorphous libertarian sexuality, but there is no reason to argue that the trend
represents powerful narcissism on the part of men while similar

women's poses represent submissive display. Plus, the canard about queers having high disposable income (perpetuated by Justice Antonin Scalia of the U.S. Supreme Court, among many others) has been criticized for its blindness to class, race, and gender distinctions: For queers, "being everywhere" includes poverty programs as much as boardrooms.[30]

But thanks to commodification of the male subject, men are brought out into the bright light of narcissism and purchase. In related developments, men's striptease shows performed for female audiences (extremely rare up to the 1970s) reference not only changes in the direction of power and money, but also a public site where "women have come to see exposed male genitalia; they have come to treat male bodies as objects only." During the 1998 men's World Cup of Soccer, the French Sexy Boys Band offered special strip shows for *"les filles sans foot"* ("girls without soccer/girls who couldn't care less"). The band has been performing in Paris since 1993 to sell-out crowds: Its all-female audiences must book two weeks in advance. And the U.S. Chippendales (established in 1978) toured northern Europe in the spring and summer of 1999 to crowds of women—*The Full Monty* (1997) writ large, even though some female spectators found the reversal of subject positions far from easy. The group markets its own merchandise and licenses its name. The North American middle-class labor market now sees wage discrimination by beauty among men as much as women, and major corporations frequently require executives to tailor their body shapes to the company ethos—or, at least, encourage employees to cut their weight in order to reduce health-care costs to the employer. In 1998, 93 percent of U.S. companies featured related health programs programs for workers, compared with 76 percent in 1992.

Figures from the American Academy of Cosmetic Surgery indicate that men had more than 6,500 face-lifts and 680,000 other cosmetic procedures in 1996. In 1997, men accounted for a quarter of all such procedures, and the following year straight couples were frequently scheduling surgery together (up 15 percent in a year). Between 1996 and 1998, cosmetic surgery among men increased 34 percent, mostly for liposuction (which has quadrupled since 1990). Gay men reportedly often use steroids for cosmetic purposes, and a third of all "graying" male U.S. workers in 1999 colored their hair to counter the effect of aging on their careers. Midtown Manhattan now offers specialists in ear, hand, and foot waxing, with men making up 40 percent of the clientele. In 1997, men's toiletries were a $3.5 billion market in the United States. Young men are beginning to experience the somato-mimetic problems of young women—and no wonder. Consider *Playgirl* magazine. Its male centerfolds have undergone comprehensive transformations over the past quarter-century: The average model has lost twelve pounds of fat and gained twenty-five pounds of muscle. GI Joe dolls of the 1960s had biceps to a scale of 11.5 inches, an average dimension. In 1999, their biceps were at a scale of 26 inches, beyond that of any recorded bodybuilder. Similar changes have been made to other dolls—*Star Wars* figures, for example. There are obvious effects. In 1997, 43 percent of American men up to their late fifties reported dissatisfaction with their appearance, compared with 34 percent in 1985 and 15 percent in 1972. Subscriptions to the bodybuilding magazine *Men's Health* went from 250,000 in 1990 to 1.5 million in 1997. The new century brought reports of 1 million men diagnosed with body dysmorphic disorder and the invention of the "Adonis Complex" by psychiatrists to account for the vastly increased numbers of eating and exercise disorders among men, which suggests that dissatisfaction with the body has crossed genders: Sixty percent of eating disorders in the United States are now reported by women, and 40 percent are reported by men. There has even been growth in the discourse of feelings: In 1988, one-third of callers to Britain's national telephone counseling service were men. In 1998, men accounted for more than half the calls.[31] What Ellen Tien calls "the rising tide of male vanity" has real costs to conventional maleness.[32]

Consider the turnaround of Australian rugby league—the "working-man's game" that both drew on and inscribed suburban and rural working-class and Roman Catholic masculinity throughout most of eastern Australia for the first seventy years of the twentieth century. Rugby league was dying in the early '80s. Clubs were losing money, crowds were down, merchandise was not being sold, and the schools could not condone requiring young men to play so violent and unprotected a sport. The *Sydney Morning Herald* published an editorial in 1983 charging the game with a "thuggery" that locked it in "a 1950s time-warp." As happened in the NFL a decade later, much rough play was forced out of the sport. This was in keeping with rugby league's self-civilizing mission to win back mothers, Catholic schools, and TV ratings by eradicating most of the violence: "Players with evil reputations were rubbed out." People started allowing their students and sons to play rugby league again. TV ratings and attendance at games increased. For some, this represented a loss. The trade publication *Rugby League Week* ran a 1990 cover story entitled, "WIMPS: Is the Modern Forward Going Soft?" in which an interviewer asked whether "the men were as hard as they once were." The interviewee Les Davidson, a former teammate of Ian Roberts (more about him later), claimed that "wimps" had "wormed" their way into the national side. Men whom it might be assumed "had guts" in fact "went to water" under physical intimidation.[33]

The renewal of rugby league involved an attempt to sexualize the game as a hook for straight women and gay men, because they fall into cohorts with high discretionary income. A formerly exclusive address to straight men was redirected to other niche markets. Rugby league's 1980s reforms included the arrival of a marketing manager who aimed to "get away from the game's 'thugby' league image and promote the players as fit, skilled athletes." The TV audience went up 10 percent in 1989 (including a 21 percent increase among women) after a pre-season promotional video with Tina Turner was released; the game's officials described the video as part of "a ballsy campaign that appealed to women and young men ... and reached into the white-collar audience without alienating league's traditional blue-collar supporter base." The game's general manager, John Quayle, argued for the commercials because the players with Turner were "good-looking, they're sexy." Sexy to whom, and how would he know? The answer came in an interview with the *Australian Financial Review* in which Quayle explained that Turner is "sexy" and the men have "sex appeal" because they "play a physical sport that relates to her performance." By 1993, 30 percent of rugby league's TV audience was female. Of course, this has not meant an end to the aura of rugged straight masculinity surrounding the sport. The Fox television network promotes rugby league as "High-speed chases. Spectacular collisions. Explosive conflicts. No stuntmen." For some feminist critics, rugby league will never escape condemnation as "simply a form of legitimised violence."[34] But this period also saw the emergence of intertextual, mocking radio and TV sports shows, such as the Australian Broadcasting Corporation's women-driven *Live and Sweaty*, that played with objectification of players' bodies.

So where is HM now? To make that question all the queerer, the remainder of this chapter is dedicated to two studies of sportsmen whose media history complicates Connell's accounts, bracketed by an analysis of gays in sport.

A Man Named Armstrong Meets Laurie Lawrence

"Does it hurt?" —*Laurie Lawrence, swimming coach*
    "Yeah, it bloody hurts." —*Swimmers*
    "Does it hurt as much as this?" —*Lawrence, running his knuckles across a brick wall until they bleed*

Most Australian sport stars, from animals (generally racehorses) to boxers, cricketers, and soccer players, have been male. Only in tennis and the summer Olympics have women taken their place, albeit still subordinated to men in terms of opportunities, rewards, and myth-making. Yet despite a pattern of allocating attention and resources to men's sports, and the vastly greater numbers of men chosen for the Olympics, Australian women have done much better at the Games, especially since World War II. And Australian men have been spectacularly unsuccessful at most modern Olympics since 1976. As one of the three countries that has been represented at each modern Olympiad, with vast amounts of public money spent on elite athletics in the quest for a national image, this failure matters.[35]

The lack of fit between the allocation of resources and the achievement of Olympic success derives from the country's culture of masculinity, itself a byproduct of an aberrant demographic history: Until well into the twentieth century, men far outnumbered women in post-invasion Australia (after 1770). The proportion of married people was exceptionally low because of a heavily male immigration pattern during the convict period (1788–1840) combined with the devastating global depression of 1890 and World War I mortality. The ratio of men to women was slightly higher than 2:1 in 1840. And it took until 1980 for the ratio to fall to just under 1:1. These figures make for a deficit in equality and everyday cultural norms. From the first period of colonial settlement in 1788, sport was ineffably male, linked initially to drinking houses and the public violence of working men, and later to a cross-class, biologistic notion of masculinity. This discourse grew in power and complexity as connections were adduced during the nineteenth century among vitality, rurality, and the whiteness of Australian-born men, known as "cornstalks." Local virility was much remarked on in the newspapers, especially with the advent of sculling in the 1850s and the popularity of swimming from the 1890s.[36] Masculinity made sports a key arena for differentiating the white Australian nation from Britain and the rest of the world, a differentiation that has been carried forward since by public mythology, government programs and propaganda, international image, media attention, and everyday talk.

This is especially interesting in the pool. The fact that water is open to both sexes leads to a certain androgyny, and swimming has always been considered appropriate for women in Australia. Although they endured gender segregation in swimming holes and pools, Victorian and Edwardian commentary remarked approvingly that submerged female bodies were mostly hidden at the point of exertion and did not produce unsightly sweat. The argument for women's swimming was contingent on proving that they were not "animated by unworthy intent," as some municipal officials feared.[37] Yet over time, the increasingly near-nakedness involved, and the languorous connotations of still water, have accreted the activity with "suspect" meanings.

Unstable gender identities are at work here. We can see them in the identification of swimming with homoeroticism, as per Duncan Grant's famous 1911 painting *Bathing*, which shows young men frolicking naked in the waters. Among gay sportsmen, swimming occupies an ambiguous place. On the one hand, it is regarded as masculine because of its self-sufficiency and demands for fitness, strength, and skill. On the other, the sport's lack of intersubjective violence, and the practice of shaving the legs and torso, mark it out from body-contact games and can lead to a "faggy" reputation for college swimmers. Gay swim meets play this up, often featuring a "pink flamingo relay" in which team members wear plastic flamingo hats and pull each other along, one kicking and the other stroking. When the U.S. Olympic swimmer Melvin Stewart was featured by NBC pumping iron at the 1992 Games in Barcelona, he offered: "swimmers don't really need to do this. I do this purely for aesthetic reasons, to look better so I can pick up chicks."[38] Ambiguity again, as "wannabe" philandering is acknowledged as aesthetic self-styling. Stewart's macho bodybuilding compensates for the androgyny of his championship sport.

Let's pursue the case of male swimmers at the Olympics—an ambiguous sport for gender and nation. There they are, cocks outlined in form-hugging briefs, body hair trimmed for minimal drag, lean, leggy, ducking, diving, turning, and speeding, seemingly oblivious to the gaze of others and the actions of fellow competitors. Bug-eyed in goggles, they show muscle strain with each eruption from the water. Our vision of these swimmers comes from a multitude of angles—warming up, swimming (seen from above and below the water), atop the podium in victory, and shivering in interviews.

The uncomfortable sense of the male body straining while almost naked can lead to interesting practices of compensation in the media. The BBC has seen the perils to conventional masculinity incipient here: Instructions to its camera operators for the 1976 Games in Montreal emphasized the need to capture swimmers' "straight lines" in order to suggest "strength, security, vitality and manliness" rather than capture the "grace and sweetness" of "curved lines." NBC commentators at the Barcelona pool in 1992 referred to the "prettiness" of female competitors rather than their speed, called them "girls," and used first names to identify them. The treatment of male swimmers was radically different.[39] Ambivalence about the manliness of the swimmer is at play as well in the elite, heteronormative side to swimming, as we shall see in the case of Duncan Armstrong.

Armstrong won the men's 200 meter freestyle race at the 1988 Olympics in Seoul. Australia's only male gold-medalist in the Games, Armstrong is now a member of the International Swimming Hall of Fame. His victory was achieved in a highly tactical and controversial way—by "surfing." This technique, pioneered at the 1976 Games by the American swimmer Brian Goodell, involves swimming just behind and very close to the man in the next lane, using his drag to get a "free ride," then passing him in the last few strokes of the race. The controversy around "surfing" derives from a sense that this is not a simple swim-off (although "dragging" is, of course, an accepted technique in bike races). Armstrong swam a "smart" race. There was nothing instinctive here. This was a carefully planned and executed manipulation of circumstance by a swimmer who was simultaneously an industrial subject and object: schooled in the physics of drag, disciplined, and self-controlled. But TV commentary on the race betrayed traces of an erotic side to the event in addition to its mechanics. Channel 10, which broadcast the Games in Australia, covered women's gymnastics by juxtaposing a viscerally sexist male enthusiast (Tim Webster) with a carefully observant female expert (Frances Crampton). Consider this discussion about one competitor: "She is certainly cute, that little Chinese girl—she looks like she'd break if she landed too hard" (Webster) and "Cheng is in fact the smallest girl in the competition, standing at just 143 centimeters and weighing a mere 36 kilos" (Crampton). But when Armstrong swam, this opposition broke down. Male race callers fell into an orgiastic frenzy that an Australian man had finally won something. "Oh my God, oh my God, oh my God," shrieked Channel 10's commentator as Armstrong touched the wall for the final time. Remind you of anything? This is, then, a world of contradictions—bizarre testimony to the complexities of so-called male rationality versus the phenomenon of "high arousal for announcers" noted by communications research.[40] The swimmer's body had become an object of desire in this coverage, consumed by the gaze of the announcer and the audience.

In 1989, Armstrong posed for a color supplement in Brisbane's *Sunday Mail* newspaper. In the photo, he is lying in rushing water, costumed in blue trunks, face smiling, elbows up, buttocks sloping away to the shallows. Anybody for centerfolds? (A decade later, he could be found as one of Stuart Spence's photographic portraits, this time naked to the navel save for epaulettes and dark glasses.) Inside the 1989 supplement, Armstrong is photographed with his (then) partner and his sports car at the University of Florida—wages of the NCAA's investment in draining brawn from across the globe. "As long as I'm swimming I'm marketable," he told the *Mail* reporter; "as long as I'm breaking world records, I'm even more marketable."[41] Armstrong shifts between the unstable position of the body on display, defenseless before the gaze, and the administrative figure of shrewd self-commodification, in control. His portrait reveals fissures in the representation of masculinity, occasioned by the pressure to make men visually appealing, to play up their beauty as part of selling their sporting maleness. The graceless antinomies of fey swimmer and tough organization man are crucial to the latter-day work of being a sportsman, with the complex connection of these subjectivities referenced in Armstrong's slippage between a self submerged in water and mired in managerialism: "We swam such and such a time. . . . Oh, I mean Laurie and I." Who is Laurie?

Sons, Lovers, Lawrence/Dunkin' Laurie

There is something special about Laurie Lawrence. An indefinable quality which sets him apart—a quality of the human spirit which embodies trust and motivates those around him to give of their very best. . . . His impact on the business community has been quite spectacular. He has proven to be uniquely capable of drawing clear parallels between business success and high sporting achievement.
—Promotion for Australia's Nationwide Realty National Convention (1996)

Armstrong's coach, Laurie Lawrence, also a Hall of Famer, drew more attention from the Australian media during the Seoul Games than his charge. Lawrence's body and its psyche were depicted, slowed down, speeded up, and analyzed over and over again on news and sports programs. This was a response to bizarre conduct. As Armstrong stood on the winner's podium, Lawrence screamed down at him, crying out pathetically for recognition: "Dunc, Dunc, turn around. I know you, Dunc." Then he sprinted poolside (pursued by pulsating Australian news crews) and broke through security to dive, fully clothed (Bermuda shorts, Hawaiian shirt, and slouch hat), into the pool. At other points, this histrionic figure shouted, "He did it," "We did it," and "My boy." He

was even wont to refer to Armstrong as "the animal" or "the bas-
tard" (used here as terms of endearment).

As replays treated us to the coach's odd conduct in slow motion,
commentators endorsed the behavior as wild but also beautifully
controlled: "He wanted to swear, but he didn't" was a representative remark. Even the TV talk-show host Clive Robertson, the
one critical voice, merely inquired what kind of parents would
name their child Laurence Lawrence. This is something of a paradox: Attention is paid to Lawrence because he is out of control,
but he is admired because he is under control.

The relationship between Lawrence and Armstrong was presented as a grand rogue egging on his pseudo-son. This image dis-
torted Lawrence's competence as a successful administrator. The
picture of a harmless eccentric effectively obscured the reality of
his skills in scientific management, time discipline, and business
acumen—all qualities required of the contemporary professional
sports coach. For behind the lovable, fallible, hysterical Australian
man functioning in a carnivalesque manner stands a clever disci-
plinarian. Coaches must know about health, dietetics, vitamins,
training schedules, promotion, intrasport politics, swimming techniques and rules, and governmental and commercial contingen-
cies—in short, the forms of discipline that produce sporting success. Control over the quotidian activities of their charges
frequently extends to personal relationships—older male coaches
as Svengalis. Despite Laurie Lawrence's "cowboy" persona, his
Web site proudly notes his four college qualifications and his role
as a front-cover icon for the magazine *Inside Business Success*.[42]

Armstrong himself became a vocal supporter of coaches' inde-
pendence from the wider sports bureaucracy, referring to their
"individual rights to coach in the way they want." But Lawrence's
cool eye found no place for "Dunc" in his mid-'90s list of great
swimmers.[43] The loyalty of coach to swimmer is contingent on the
former's exercise of his prerogative to forget emotion and engage
in a clinical ranking. Perhaps because of this, Armstrong told one

caller in an on-line discussion during the 2000 Olympics that he was competing in "beer-swilling" and "staying-up-lating" contests and said that Lawrence "on television is actually a lot softer than he is real life. . . . He just doesn't understand—when it's not the same for everyone."[44]

It should come as no surprise that Lawrence was named Australian Achiever of the Year in 1988 and won an Advance Australia Award. Promoted as "Lawrence of Australia" in advertisements, he is described as the "Master Motivator" who inspires audiences with "Aussie parochialism and good humour." Such representations blend a crass nationalism and narrow-mindedness with optimism and good nature, suggesting that Lawrence's life is lived in the name of a joke. The modern managerialism of sport, which is often actively opposed to worker solidarity and welfare, is made to seem as if it is about patriotism and a few laughs with the lads. But such a message reinforces the exclusivity of the clubhouse—women, transsexuals, and gays seem unwelcome. Yet the representations of Armstrong as an object of the gaze, and Lawrence as a hysterical man, complicate this message of Australian sporting masculinity. And more confusion is coming.

Gays and Sport: Don't Be, Don't Tell

This glittering metropolis [Sydney] could conceivably be described as the camp capital of the universe, if only because Sydney-siders enjoy more drag cabaret per capita than any other city in the world. . . . Except, of course, when everyone's too busy ogling the homoerotic spectacle of professional football. —P. Cahill (1997, 44)

The magazine *xy* calls sports "the last closet."[45] Despite the "pink dollar" market and other commercial determinations, enormous barriers confront gay and lesbian athletes (see also Chapter 4). The U.S. Olympic Committee sued the Gay Games over ownership of the Olympic name in the Supreme Court in 1987 and placed the home of the games' founder Tom Waddell, a decathlete who competed in the 1968 Olympic Games in Mexico City, under lien as he was dying. It did not take such actions against the Police, Diaper, or Dog Olympics. The media have hardly been friendly—when the heterosexual ABC telecaster Dick Schaap wrote an obituary on Waddell for *Sports Illustrated*, the editors deleted a reference to his kissing the decathlete farewell, and the Montreal media, which had talked up the city's unsuccessful bid for the 2002 Games as a moneymaker, did not cover local athletes' results at the 1998 event in Amsterdam. At the same time, this may have encouraged the Gay Games' inclusive ethos—you don't have to be gay to participate, and no minimum level of competence is required. The notion is of a contest with one's own record as much as against others, to meet as well as defeat.[46]

Locker-room argot in elite sports is resolutely misogynistic, gay-hating, and excoriatingly evaluative of differences between men. The media also have a poor record. Jim Rome, host of an interview show on Fox and a nationally syndicated talk-back radio program, is promoted on TV using tape of a famous on-camera incident: The U.S. football player Jim Everett of the New Orleans Saints assaulted Rome because Rome repeatedly referred to him during their interview as "Chris Evert," a slight occasioned by the claim that Everett was prone to "avoiding hits."[47]

Twenty years ago, the NFL's David Kopay became the first major sportsman to come out, in the hope that this would improve matters for others. His 1975 autobiography made the best-seller list of the *New York Times*, but the paper did not review it, and a column about the book written by the Pulitzer Prize winner Dave Anderson was rejected by management. Today, Kopay claims that many on-field brawls still result from players' being called "fag," a sign of continued intolerance. Kopay was out to many teammates, finding particular solace from African Americans, whose knowledge of straight white male bigotry made them excellent confidants. He says that obstacles lie with franchise owners, who believe openly gay players will lose them money through diminished sponsorship and ratings. Kopay calls for football associations and players' unions to issue a civil-rights statement of support for gay athletes and provide assistance to high-school and college players, whose suicide rates are high. When a young high-school football star came out in 2000, it became front-page news across the country, so transgressive was this statement.[48]

The Advocate, a gay and lesbian magazine, ran a 1996 cover story entitled "Inside the NFL Closet: Why Pro Football Players Can't Come Out." It quotes major media commentators explaining that gay and lesbian football fans may have to wait to claim another out football player: It is felt that life on and off the field, and endorsement issues, make such moves impractical. But rumors about players are intense. While gay fans want to out players who are in the closet, so do their straight opponents. The former Dallas Cowboys quarterback Troy Aikman is subject to much innuendo, as both proponents and critics seek to claim him. His former coach Barry Switzer allegedly told a journalist: "I have to take so much shit off that kid, and he's gay." Aikman's denials are lost on many audiences. It is claimed that gay football players have extensive clauses in their contracts prescribing public behavior and prohibiting attendance at gay bars. The NFL agent Leigh Steinberg "has indicated that it is easier to win endorsement deals for an athlete who has committed a felony than for one who has committed fellatio," while coaches doubt the suitability of gays as football players. "You try to sell your team on being a tough, rough, hard-nosed football team and I assume if someone was of that persuasion, I am not sure of his toughness," said Johnny Roland, running-back coach for the Arizona Cardinals during the cable network ESPN's 1998 special "Gays in Sports." In 1998, the Green Bay Packers "hero" Reggie White appeared suited up in newspaper advertisements paid for by the Christian right against gays in sport. This drew some criticism—notably, from the Minnesota Vikings player Robert Smith—but the only official reaction from the NFL was to criticize the use of a football uniform without the league's consent.[49]

Baseball also has done little to address gays in sports, although the San Francisco Giants have held a Gay and Lesbian Day at their ballpark. Cricket is rife with homophobia. The former West Indian cricket captain Brian Lara is heckled by his own team's supporters as "pooch" and by white Australian opponents as "Princess." We all know about the anxiously repeated insistence that the NBA superstar Earvin "Magic" Johnson did not contract HIV from a homosexual encounter (see Chapter 3). The Team England soccer player Justin Fashanu hanged himself after he came out and was accused of having sex with underage boys. Brian Clough, Fashanu's manager at Nottingham Forest, learned in 1980 that the player was frequenting the local gay scene. Referring to him as "a bloody poof," Clough suspended Fashanu and called the police to escort him from practice. When Fashanu came out to the tabloids in 1990, he was criticized by some gay activists for commercial self-interest and attacked by the black media and his brother, fellow soccer player John Fashanu, who offered him thousands of pounds to hide his identity and did not speak to him for the last seven years of his life: "I wouldn't like to play in the same team as him or even get changed in the vicinity of him." The tabloids were quick to attack Justin Fashanu over the accusations of sexual assault, inviting other "victims" to contact the press. When he died, they stated that he had killed himself after "a final orgy of homosexual lust" before ending his guilt, despite disavowals from the sauna where he had spent his last hours and the fact that there was no warrant for his arrest. Soccer held no memorial service.[50]

Other soccer players have gone through years of taunting. In the 1980s, Chelsea's Pat Nevin became "dubious" in the eyes of his teammates because he listened to Joy Division rather than Lionel Richie. Today, the Team England and Chelsea fullback Graeme Le Saux (promoted as a straight husband, father, art-gallery afficionado, and *Guardian* reader, whose wife has a sociology degree and reads Gabriel García Marquez) is considered "suspect" because of his interest in art and antiques (perhaps this is a displacement of class antagonism). He has routinely been jeered by crowds. In 1999, Le Saux and a Team England colleague, Liverpool's Robbie Fowler, became involved in an on-field dispute when Fowler repeatedly referred to Le Saux as "poof" and "faggot," then turned his buttocks toward Le Saux and shouted: "Come on, come on; give it to me up the arse." Le Saux complained to match officials, and they penalized him for wasting time. When Fowler said, "Fuck your family," Le Saux knocked him to the ground, subsequently apologizing. Fowler's failure to reciprocate shocked the Professional Footballers' Association. British Sports Minister Tony Banks urged gay players to come out, adding, "I have to admit that it would be a very, very brave footballer who admits he is gay and then goes out on the pitch."[51]

The only Olympic gold-medal swimmer on the gay list is Hayes. After Greg Louganis, the multiple Olympic gold-medal-winning diver, came out, a U.S. state senator tried to prevent him from speaking at the University of Southern Florida on the grounds that it would "promote homosexuality" and "moral decadence." Female colleagues once stuffed a gerbil with its legs tied together in Louganis's sports bag at a competition, while male rivals formed a "Beat the Faggot Club"—on par with U.S. talk-show host Arsenio Hall's remark, "If we can put a man on the moon, why can't we get one on Martina Navratilova?" Instead of hiring Louganis during its coverage of the Atlanta Games, NBC offered analysts who had never made it to the top ten or were one-off successes. David Pichler, who followed Louganis as the United States' number-one diver, has run into bizarre abuse since he announced his homosexuality: His former coach sought restraining orders to keep the Pichler's boyfriend away from himself and his son. But the sport now sees a lot of people coming out, despite taunts from straights, and Louganis did not lose support from Speedo or other sponsors. The extreme athlete Rodger McFarlane believes he has maintained and developed relationships with sponsors beyond his physical peak precisely because he is gay. Rudy Galindo, the U.S. national figure-skating champion in 1996, is publicly gay, as are the bodybuilders Gene Kuffel, Mr. USA International 1997, and Bob Paris, a former Mr. America who was married to his boyfriend during his tenure. Paris suffered jibes from other competitors. Increasing numbers of high-school and college athletes are out on the Internet, thanks to its combination of publicness and privacy. The bulk of impressionistic opinion says that coming out, once perhaps harder for athletes than anyone else, is becoming much easier.[52]

Some openness to sexual diversity may derive from the 1970s uptake of built bodies by gay men, a fascinating counter to the long-held sense that, as *Outrage* magazine put it, sports are high on the list of "things and jobs that poofters can't/won't do." For Brian Pronger, the cultural fix of sports relates to sexual identity in historically uneven ways. There was a time when his "sense of being a gay man had more to do with witty conversations at elegant dinner parties than it did with grunting and sweating in a gym." But the buff-bodied gay man became so powerful as a categorial that, by the '80s, having huge muscles sometimes coded men as homosexual—the V-shaped torso, washboard abdominal musculature, and bulging biceps of the "muscle queen." In the early '90s, the Australian gay magazine *Campaign* ran a story on "the rise of gay footy."[53]

Of course, this change produced—in Gay Games advertising, for example—a neat, clean, beatified, sanitary signification of lesbianism and homosexuality that is associated with sporting prowess and over-compensation to counter the older categorial of effeminate physical insufficiency. Such appropriation of musculature can be criticized as an "unself-conscious adoption of a patriarchal, often misogynist masculinity," with the Gay Games endorsing—and profiting from—a focus on "a certain urban, upwardly mobile, gay-male consumerist mentality" that privileges a limited array of somatotypes and objectifies men. It bought into parts of dominant masculinity, becoming doubly an affront and an exemplification: Although gay men appropriated conventional signifiers of male power, thereby destabilizing a straight monopoly, they were also further typifying such forms of life as the acme of maleness. This hypermasculinity hardened emotions and bodies—a tribute to the very models that had traditionally excluded and brutalized gays. But it was equally "a parodic representation of masculinity," playfully troping musculature in "a kind of drag." We could view this either as seizing the signage to counter categorials or as a gruesome throwback to racist and fascist imagery (a particular affront to gay black men).[54]

Clearly, this is a time of great contradiction—which is precisely where we meet Ian Roberts, admiringly described by *Campaign* as a "hit-load of raw physical power."[55] A star of rugby league, "the working-man's game," Roberts came from a class background that made the choice to engage in parody improbable—and the opportunity to activate gay desires even more so.

Ian Roberts—Prop Forward

All the "hunks" of [rugby] league are gathered in a carpark known as The Spit. The aim is to show off the musclemen of the game to an adoring female audience. The irony is that the place they chose is one of the most notorious gay "beats" in Australia. —R. Sleeman (1990, 14)

For a century there was nothing about gay sportsmen in the Australian press, and lesbians gained attention only in panic-laden conversion narratives about young women.[56] This changed in the mid-1990s, when massive publicity was given to Ian Roberts's coming out.

Roberts is pictured on the cover of his authorized biography, *Finding Out.* The space from chin to hairline occupies the page, fingers spread across his mouth and jaw and eyes fixed on a point in the distance. This is a pensive Roberts, weighing the pros and cons of a professional rugby-league player declaring his homosexuality (the image equally calls up the poet pondering the infinite or a polar explorer wondering which clothes to pack). But on the spine and back cover, the image is quite different. A half-body shot from the waist up, unclothed, muscles taught, veins visible, and pectorals bulging, is on the cusp of bodybuilding and eroticism. Other photographs in the book veer between happy family snapshots and Roberts in leather gear or posing naked for a gay magazine. This is quite a contrast with his colleague from the national team, Andrew Ettingshausen, who sued the Australian Consolidated Press for showing his penis in a women's magazine on the grounds that such sexualization threatened his income.[57]

Roberts is a front-row forward, or prop, in rugby league, still the most systematically daunting and rugged sport I know after boxing, automobile racing, and ice hockey (the last of which now has thriving queer leagues in Canada and the United States). In recalling his adolescence, the journalist Peter Wilkins wrote, "Other footballing codes were mere flyweight warm-ups compared to the chin to boots jarring of the heavyweight League match." The principal goal was "to instil fear and to inflict pain." Wilkins recounts admiringly the case of a player who stayed on the field in a premiership match in 1990 despite serious damage to his cruciate ligament, offering (almost as an afterthought) that the man's knee "never fully recovered and he slipped from top-grade view." This self-destructive heroism is integral to the ethos of the game, a frightening testimony to the post-career value placed on working-class sportsmen.

Props such as Roberts need to be able to tackle other big forwards, run with the ball, pass it to colleagues, and support the hooker (the player who strikes for the ball with his foot) in scrums (though this last skill has become less important since the 1980s). Kevin Ryan, a famous prop, says, "The only secret to success is to be fit and hard," and Roberts has long been known for what the working-class *Mirror* newspaper has called "bone-crunching hits."[58]

In his brief introduction to his biography, Roberts makes an interestingly Foucauldian use of truth as a technique for living, a method of becoming free and fulfilled. Telling the truth about his sexual practices is not a moral obligation but part of his relationship to himself. The moral part comes in his desire for others to come out and join him in providing "the gay role models that future generations of Australians truly and obviously need." The book proper begins with a set of epistolary confessions, a compilation of public reactions to his coming out, offered in montage form using different typefaces. These include encouragement from a seventy-year-old gay lapsed prop, tales of sex with international players, support from straights, confusion from teenage players, and denigration from a former professional athlete who "had a brush with this so-called lifestyle" and warns Roberts that hellfire awaits should he continue to be gay. We move on to the Roberts family's history, including the one moment in the book I actually found perverse: How could a sane seven-year-old actually kiss a poster of a Bay City Roller?[59]

Ian Roberts was having secret sex with boys from a young age. By the time he discovered the taunts made by school students about homosexuality, he was already sleeping with prominent young sportsmen. The prevailing presumption as he grew up was that sexual practice could be read from size and demeanor; as a large star rugby league player, Roberts could only be straight. His teen years were in other ways typical of working-class Australian white men. Packed with violence, they involved a strong sense of turf and pride, with weekend evenings commonly given over to territorial and personal battles. Fighting was both a rite of passage and a physical necessity. From that point, the story focuses on wondering how rugby league could fit with being gay and whether his parents would accept a homosexual son. There are twists and turns along the way: personal and business disasters, horrendous playing injuries, and anti-gay and intra-gay violence quite apart from battles on the field. The tales of everyday advice from teammates are galling, encouraging Roberts to bite and kick opponents and regard them as barely human.[60] The book covers the days when the brutal coach Roy Masters, trumpeting his psychology degree, instructed players to slap each other in the face as a warm-up. (It is interesting that after failing to win a competition as a coach, Masters continued to contribute to Australian maleness via a regular newspaper column in which he famously wrote on one occasion of the collective beauty and rugged individualism of Australian soldiers).

These developments took place across Roberts's career, but his special reputation for toughness endured. Coworkers dealt with rumors about his sexuality in interesting ways. George Piggins, one of his first coaches at South Sydney and a former international player, is quoted as saying: "It's got to be a defect to be born with the makings of a man and the emotions of a woman. But it doesn't mean you don't have the same rights as everyone else." This is hardly a positive embrace of Roberts's subjectivity, and it is not phrased in the polite social-constructionist terms of the educated middle class, but Piggins does acknowledge the issue of equal rights. The South Sydney tradition of poverty and social distress bred people who were used to hard times and understood life on the margin, generally through aboriginality or class background. But when Roberts announced plans to leave the club for wealthy rival Manly-Warringah—long known for buying young players from Souths—former teammates started to criticize him for his sexuality, and crowds engaged in ritual abuse, in keeping with the virulent bigotry many sports fans exhibit toward gay men. Attempts to commodify his image via the *Ian Roberts Total Energy* poster book countered this scuttlebutt by featuring (unacknowledged) his sister in the background, and he typically told reporters he had girlfriends.[61]

When he finally came out, Roberts received much support from colleagues—he refers to rugby league as "an incredibly accepting community"—and some savage treatment. The gay press was the same, with accusations that he came out in order to make himself more marketable. But Roberts also mentions that rugby league officials did not attempt to make him hide his sexual preference (unlike, it seems, the NFL) and have supported him since, not least because "it took their audience to a wider audience in the community." Some of Roberts's colleagues stated that being his friend led to some abuse, but they stood by him. The *Footy Show* had a very positive interview with Roberts in which he declared that other gays played in the professional league. The program's presenters, Paul Vautin, Steve Roach, and Peter Sterling—all former players—subsequently appeared in posters supporting The Lesbian and Gay Anti-Violence Project. Roberts's macho image was confirmed by frequent use of his two favorite words: "mate" and "fuck." The month his book was published, *Rugby League Week* magazine ran a story on tough players, referring not only to Roberts's "crash-tackling form" and "ferocious front-on defence," but also to his concern for opponents. The article noted that he had never been sent from the field or suspended for rough play and listed him alongside other powerful but fair players—as opposed to those who regularly broke the rules. There is now an "Ian Roberts Tribute Page" on the World Wide Web, complete with nude shots and a series of articles about his career. He is a spokesperson for Puma and Telstra, and he models clothes for Ella Bache. He was appointed captain of his new club when his biography came out, and he has written a column on exercise and fitness for the gay magazine *Outrage*. Roberts's example has become a much-cited one for gays in the United States looking for pro players to come out. He is also an icon in France and on the global Gay.Net.[62] Gaygate.com commences with a quotation from Roberts: "There's no use in worrying about everyone else's feelings. . . . My life is my life, and they don't have a say in it."[63] Roberts's coming-out was noted by the *Economist* magazine in its survey of the impact of gay men on the Australian economy, and he features prominently in "SmartChat's" profiles of famous gays.[64]

Not surprisingly, Roberts celebrates split subjectivity, insisting that the experience of rugby league and physical violence "has nothing to do with the fact that I'm gay. Some people think everything relates to that." Damien Millar (1997) notes in his review of *Finding Out* how laughable it is to assume that we have continuous, logical, or even interlocking selves, with sexuality central to all of life. And what about anti-gay stereotypes and categorials shouted on the field? Representative remarks from Roberts include: "I don't condone it, but I don't accept that as pure hatred like I've seen prejudice displayed otherwise" and "There are some people who call you a poof and you laugh with them, while there are others who you just want to smack their heads in." In his Queensland club's official "Profile," Roberts lists his toughest opponent as "Don't Remember Her Name" and confesses he is "not partial to frocks." During the year after the book's release, Roberts received a thousand letters detailing discrimination, which he publicized as part of a campaign to have gay sex-education material distributed in public schools. In 1999, Roberts was part of a national campaign called Outlink, a support and advocacy service for young rural queers confronting suicide issues, even as he confronted charges of on-field brutality in court and a fan was convicted of stalking him.[65] When the Australian rugby league and rugby union sides were competing against England and Wales, respectively, on the same day in 2000, Roberts made a public statement to the teams, urging closeted players to come out: "Don't be ashamed of being gay."[66]

Both Armstrong and Roberts clearly find that the costs and benefits of commodification are high, and the gaze is constant and disciplined, yet seemingly spontaneous, all in the name of purchasing power and freedom. They are not alone. The *New York Times* tells us that "unauthorized videotapes of hundreds of naked male athletes in the locker rooms of more than 50 universities are being produced, sold and distributed on sexually oriented sites on the World Wide Web." In 1998, rugby-union-crazed New Zealand

saw its first gay interprovincial match.[67] Once, the straight sportsman could be promoted as an icon of his country, a proud figure
animated by patriotism. Now he is revealed as a much more contradictory figure, animated as much by a polymorphously perverse
self-display and the desire for material gain as by anything else.
The mythic national male subject—outside the reaches of capital, embodying both nature and history, an elemental agent of
progress—is revealed to be very much an object, made so by desir-
ing gazes and plastic moneys. Duncan Armstrong poses; Laurie
Lawrence motivates; Channel 10 salivates; Ian Roberts comes
out; and commodities circulate. Simmering above and below those
actions, we find the odd blend of industrial precision and gay
abandon expected of today's man. Does HM help us explain this?
Or do we need to think about a) the inevitability of stereotyping;
and b) the political economy of looking?

3

Panic Sports and the Racialized Male Body

with David Rowe and Jim McKay

Sports is one of the few bits of glue that holds society together.
—Spiro Agnew, media critic and vice-president (as quoted in Lasch 1979, 202–3)

f sex and gender putatively unite white men and men of color, then race and racism divide them. The appeal to "natural superiority" that many men make in regard to women is compromised in the history of white racist ideology, because closeness to "nature" makes black men "inferior" to their white counterparts. But the capacity to transcend nature and the limitations of the bodily world that white racist masculinity champions is occluded in the corporeally dominated realm of sport (and sex). It is here that black men not infrequently claim genetic superiority ("White men can't jump"—maybe not in the NBA, where no one jumps very high, but look over at the world of the high jump and pole vault, where truly international contests disclose a different, much whiter, much higher story). White men counter with assertions of mental and moral domination ("Blacks lack leadership skills"—maybe in U.S. sports that deny managerial roles to African Americans, but look over at the history of West Indian cricket, where Frank Worrell's and Clive Lloyd's reigns as captain disclose a much blacker, cerebrally successful story). The practice of "stacking" in sport, whereby certain roles are distributed according to assumed racial characteristics, is an attempt to reinstitute a sporting hierarchy on other than strictly corporeal grounds.[1]

The image of the black male is a dominant feature of contemporary sports culture, especially through promotions for sports goods by companies such as Nike and Reebok. Michael Jordan's iconic ascendancy has produced the contradictory outcome that the black man's body is simultaneously celebrated, when associated with sport, and feared and denounced, when connected with violent crime. The "black superstud sportsman" emerges at a time when systemic racism stimulates million-man marches and other responses to the subordination of African American men.[2]

In America today, "youth, sports, and violence" is highly racialized code for 1) a *de*scription—"black men playing college and professional football, basketball, and baseball who are unused to power and money and manifest their newfound 'privilege' in violence or as sexual abuse"; or 2) a *pre*scription—"governments and companies seeking to displace the frustrations of inner-city residents by requiring them to 'share' in 'improving' their districts and find 'appropriate' recreational pastimes to occupy themselves." In either case, the logic is discriminatory. The first account bears all the usual traces of white American anxiety about black American success. The second bears all the usual traces of property developers seeking the patina of disinterested citizenship and the reality of improved real-estate values and cheap labor.

That history predates the arrival of African American men on 1950s fields of green (as boys of summer) and 1970s fields of parquet (as boys from the 'hood) and the 1990s recognition that welfare was costing the middle classes more than they were prepared to pay. Since the first Middletown study in the 1920s found that high-school loyalties developed and class differences slackened in Muncie, Indiana, with the arrival of basketball, sports have been heralded by many functionalists for their integrative capacities: Durkheimians have correlated suicide rates with the Super Bowl and the World Series and found lower levels than at other times of the year. Men's violence is seen as a socio-biological, hormonal danger that can be pacified and redirected through sports into an appropriate sphere. But as testosterone is the hormone that takes the blame in these accounts, what do we do with the fact that it is common in women—that many women have more testosterone than many men *and* that its links to violence are uncertain?[3] Something else is going on here.

For in addition to being right, the quotation from Spiro Agnew that opens this chapter is also wrong: 1) when the *Middletown* authors went back to Indiana ten years later, debts incurred for the school stadium had made it an unpopular Depression liability; 2) during Agnew's time as vice-president, pitched battles were fought on U.S. campuses between football players and anti-war demonstrators over perceived structural homologies between the Vietnam War and college sports; 3) self-mutilation may diminish while watching sports on TV, but domestic violence is said to increase dramatically during the Super Bowl; and 4) collegiate and professional sportsmen are disproportionately likely to be charged with sexual assaults compared with the overall national rate (and disproportionately likely to be exonerated).[4] Smiling functionalists also neglect the fact that hockey, boxing, hunting, shooting, wrestling, the martial arts, most types of football, and car and motorcycle racing glamorize violence across class and racial fractions.

At a policy level, sport is inflected with ethnocentric notions of conduct that associate "delinquency" with racial minorities. Hence the NCAA's panic about so-called showboating in college football, a thinly disguised attempt to legislate away African American styles of celebration on the grounds that they are individualistic and crowd-oriented. (These are bad things in the ideology of U.S. spectator capitalism? Hello!) It is abundantly clear that this marks a historic adjustment in the norms of public masculinity. The sweep of black men into global popular culture has been accompanied, perhaps in part achieved, by "expressive improvisational behaviors and attitudes from ghettos in Oakland to Saint Louis; the verbal 'talk' and physical survival skills of the projects from Chicago to Coney Island; and the cool, calculated confidence of rural and suburban environments from Texas to Ohio."[5]

The commercial use of sports has referenced this by picking up on and trivializing civil-rights discourse and imbuing commodities with inner-city attitude (for poor African American child targets) or picket-fence anti-attitude (for affluent white child targets). The new sneaker success, Fila, signed "good-boy" Grant Hill, then a Detroit Pistons guard, as a celebrity spokesperson to make its shoes "safe" for white suburban youth, with astonishing success.[6]). If your children wear Filas, they will *not* encounter violence or homeless people; they *will* encounter healthy SAT scores. This double-sided view came into focus most dramatically during the O. J. Simpson trials. As the author Toni Morrison explains, white men had enveloped Simpson in the commodity fold of commentary and sponsorship, relishing "the comfort they felt in his company" and recalling "the beauty of his runs." Then they found "they had loved the wrong kind of man." The media turnaround from adoration to dread exemplified and amplified this tendency: "Mr. Simpson was accused of multiple murder. But he was guilty of personal treason."[7] The black passport to white status is always revocable.

The discursive racialization of sexual violence is often accompanied by a bizarre critique of women. Jeffrey Benedict's much-cited and -reported study of male athletes and violence against women drips with anti-democratic, heteronormative, and misogynistic assumptions and figures; at the same time, it lacks longitudinal analyses, random sampling, and controls for criminal history and drug use. First, the jury system is impugned: Athletes are acquitted because jurors are blinded by celebrity stature. Then athletes are said to have had "their power of self-restraint eroded by excessive sexual indulgence" and their views of women altered by playing team sports. This combination is found to produce "increasingly deviant sexual habits." Women who willingly have sex with men outside marriage are, in short, the principal cause of sexual violence, along with popular culture itself. Both are accused by Benedict of "complicity" in the "jock–groupie tango . . . the engine driving . . . an image of women as sexually compliant." Surprise, surprise: Men are beasts who need to fuck all the time, and "bad girls" who initiate sex with a variety of partners are responsible for the mistreatment of "good girls," because they encourage men to pursue "a deviant lifestyle." The same notion of "bad girls" is evident in *Sports Illustrated*'s account of professional athletes who father children in various liaisons (also discussed in a *New York Times* editorial). "Wherever there's money there are going to be women" is a refrain. The chaplain to the San Francisco Giants (baseball) and 49ers (football) refers to "women who hunt," while the NFL's "rookie orientation" program features "former NFL groupies" explaining "how they seduced players."[8] We *have* come a long way, haven't we?

Badassed, Bareassed, and Black

The transgressive, ambiguous body of the black American is best symbolized by Dennis Rodman. Renowned in the late '80s as one of the "bad boys" who hustled and bumped the Detroit Pistons to twin NBA championships, and known for his obsessive exercising after games, Rodman is now prominent not just for his peerless rebounding for the Pistons, the San Antonio Spurs, the Chicago Bulls (complete with further consecutive titles), and (briefly) the Los Angeles Lakers and Dallas Mavericks, but also for dressing in boas, frequenting bars, sleeping with Madonna ("She wasn't an acrobat, but she wasn't a dead fish either") and imagining sex with other men. Rodman is also interesting because he rejects comfortable pigeonholing by gay politicians: He says he is not in the closet; he just has not slept with men. Further complexities flow from the way he uses queer talk to trash opponents—most notoriously asking them for dates during games and drawing fouls from their hysterical reactions. This refusal to be gay, straight, or bi- asks us to think again about tight definitions of personhood in terms of sexual practice: Rodman might fuck a guy or he might not, but he would still be the best defensive rebounder in the history of the NBA. In turn, this encourages us to problematize the essentialism of the impost to come out, not to mention its ethnocentrism. Black critics argue that the white gay movement's privileging of being out has ignored the importance for many heteronormative black families of unity against racism, which could be put in doubt by such conduct.[9]

In his two books, *Bad as I Wanna Be* (with Tim Keown) and *Walk on the Wild Side* (with Michael Silver), Rodman's body is to the fore inside and outside the covers. On the front of *Bad as I Wanna Be*, he is naked astride a motorcycle, returning the viewer's gaze at his multicolored hair and tattoos. Cross-dressing images await within. The text makes provocative statements (suitably boldfaced, often in upper case or different typefaces): "Fifty percent of life in the NBA is SEX. The other fifty percent is MONEY"; "MENTALLY, I probably am bi-sexual"; and "IF MAGIC HAD A GAY RELATIONSHIP, THAT'S HIS BUSINESS." On the cover of *Walk on the Wild Side*, Rodman is painted in "animal" mode, with the back-cover excerpt reading, "I have this fantasy that I can live my life like a tiger in the jungle—eating whatever I want, having sex whenever I want, and roaming around butt naked, wild and free." Rodman consciously plays on and with discourses of black men's sports sexuality, simultaneously exploiting and subverting prevailing readings of the heterosexual super-body. He has also appeared in a cover story for *The Advocate* in which he detailed his sexual interests and enunciated a libertarian position. Rodman truly destabilizes the mainstream media discourse that sports are inherently masculine, showing that there is no necessary correspondence among maleness, physique, and conduct. At the same time, any idealized uptake of Rodman must deal with the private demons and public commodification that drive his persona. His transition into films as a buddy-movie renegade; his sadly brief association with the Lakers and Mavericks; his arrests for driving while intoxicated and (mutual) domestic violence; tales of his high living; and his brief second marriage have become part of a legend that characterizes him less as a queer icon than as a mobile monument to eccentricity and an ultimately recuperative, albeit flexible, heterosexuality.[10]

Big Bad Ben on Steroids

Ben Johnson has a new job. The perpetually troubled Canadian sprinter is broke, needs the money, and has been hired as a personal trainer by the son of Libyan leader Muammar Gadhafi. Just weeks after his third positive drug test, Johnson, 38, has been hired to whip Saad Gadhafi, the 25-year-old son of Gadhafi, into shape for the coming Libyan soccer season that is training for the 2000 African Cup of Nations and World Cup. Johnson says he has no qualms about training the son of a leader scorned by the western world. "I am not going there for political reasons. I know there will be some negative press, but I am doing it solely to help a soccer player who needs my help. This is like a breath of fresh air. I am being given another chance and I am taking it. When I travel overseas, I am always well received, and there are many people who admire me, unlike here at home, where I am not respected." *—"Johnson Trainer,"* RunnersWeb.com (www.sharondonnelly. com/running/rw_news.html), 4 December 1999

One of the biggest media sports scandals of the late twentieth century occurred in 1988 after the Canadian sprinter Ben Johnson broke the 100 meters track world record at the Olympics in Seoul, only to be disqualified and banned for taking Stanazolol, a banned steroid. In the massive controversy over performance-enhancing drugs that followed, a state-funded Canadian inquiry found that such practices were widespread and officially tolerated. Johnson claimed that every other major track athlete was using, and has since maintained that star sprinters agree to participate at major meets on the understanding they will not be tested. The bio-medical order of power in sport was revealed to be profoundly contradictory, resting on a notion of naturally "clean bodies" alongside institutionalized bodily "contamination." Arthur Kroker et al. describe these events as the "Panic Olympics," an "age of sacrificial sports" in which "the Olympics, under the pressure of the mass media, re-enter the dark domain of mythology," with ath-letes providing a "blank screen for playing out the darker passions of triumph and scapegoatism."[11]

Johnson's subsequent life ban (imposed in 1993 after he tested above the allowable testosterone level and confirmed following appeals in 1996 and 1999 and a further failed test in '99) illustrated the depth of a panic that is unrelieved even by the familiar narra-tive of detection, exposure, retribution, denial, confession, remorse, and redemption. When an arbitrator called for his reinstatement to local track and field, Athletics Canada moved to have the Ontario Superior Court confirm the ban. Johnson himself sought the chance to clear his name because, he said, various European companies would give him sponsorship deals across a host of industries, regard-less of whether he raced again, provided that his name was cleared. His former sponsor Diadora reportedly held $100 million (Cana-dian) of his clothing line in storage, ready to release.[12]

The Canadian media had initially reacted to Johnson's victory in Seoul by stressing the symbolic significance of defeating Carl Lewis. Lewis represented all the self-confidence and power of the United States in its ordinary dealings with the "second North America." But after the disqualification, the Canadian media quickly attenuated Johnson's Canadianness, foregrounding instead his Jamaican origins. Frank Edwards, a cartoonist with the *Kingston Whig-Standard*, captured the moment with three drawings of the sprinter, captioned, respectively, "Canadian Wins Gold Medal," "Jamaican-Canadian Accused of Steroid Use," and "Jamaican Stripped of Gold Medal." While Johnson maintained that he had been expelled because "I beat the Americans," he also vowed never to race for Canada again.[13]

The next Canadian to be disqualified in the Olympics for drug use was Ross Rebagliati, a white snowboarder who won a gold medal at the 1998 Winter Games. Unlike Johnson, Rebagliati had his medal restored to him following a massive political and media campaign in Canada that featured Richard Pound, an executive board member of the International Olympic Committee. A decade earlier, Pound had recused himself from the Johnson case, but the same conflict of interest apparently did not disqualify him from defending a white athlete. Meanwhile, as Johnson's body plainly shrank to pre-steroid proportions, much was made of his figurative as well as his literal diminution, with the runner literally reduced to racing against horses and cars for publicity, reminding many African Americans of the way that Jesse Owens ran against horses after the 1936 Olympics for the amusement of whites and later turned into a supine assimilationist who was despised by radical athletes of the 1960s.[14]

The Ben Johnson story offers two lessons: that the elite sporting body is susceptible to, and partially constituted by, manipulation, and that such interventions may be performatively effective, if strictly unethical. This loss of innocence provoked a deeper anxiety about the threat to corporeal integrity posed by high-performance sports, an ontological insecurity produced by the implosion of self and other. Yet such uncertainties are licensed by coaches such as Laurie Lawrence—"caring professionals" who are dedicated to the maximization of corporeal efficiency and whose training regimens colonize sporting bodies.[15] The scandal of performance-enhancing-drug detection is seen to lie not in the intrusion of the public gaze into private life, a traditional concern of civil liberties, but in public revelations about celebrities. The detection of recreational (that is, non-sports-related) drug use has been of greater widespread concern than the invasion of privacy occasioned by the naming of players and their conduct.

Some condemnation of performance-enhancing drugs in sports concerns breaching sex and gender boundaries. Female Chinese swimmers are pejoratively described as male by some commentators, while much is also made of the feminizing effects on men of steroid use. In the case of Johnson, there was great consternation among his entourage when it was discovered that "after years of hormone drug doping he had developed an enlarged left breast. He was turning into a woman!" So Johnson engaged in two transgressions. The first was to be caught taking drugs, thereby compromising his "natural" attributes through the use of "artificial" substances. The second was to problematize his masculinity through the side effects of introduced hormones. Ironically, one of the cover stories Johnson had developed in case of detection was that he was using Probenecid—a well-known steroid-masking agent—to enhance the effectiveness of penicillin in treating gonorrhea. The sexual and racial anxiety that Johnson provoked as a successful black man at the peak of his career was to some degree discharged by his fall from grace, even as the life sentence went beyond what a murderer might expect to draw from Canadian authorities. Johnson is, to quote Stuart Hall, "both an amazing athlete, winner and record-breaker, *and* the athlete who was publicly disgraced"—hero and villain, with each status racialized.[16] The opposite phenomenon was evident following the announcement that Magic Johnson was HIV-positive.

Magic, HIV/AIDS, and (Hetero)Sexual Athletics

Upon the fields of friendly strife are sown the seeds which, on other days, on other fields, will bear the seeds of victory. —*Douglas MacArthur, football theorist and army general, 1950s (as quoted in Lasch 1979, 202)*

In November 1991, Magic Johnson called a press conference (in order to pre-empt a move by the popular media) to announce that he was HIV-positive. The intensity of the reaction was similar to that generated by the Ben Johnson affair three years earlier.[17] In this case, corporeal jeopardy stemmed not from the calculated injection of drugs, but from the unwitting transmission of a virus through sexual contact. The "globalizing panic"[18] resulting from HIV and AIDS is, according to Judith Williamson, an acute anxiety about the condition of social and bodily systems: "What seems particularly threatening about AIDS is that it is linked to the breakdown of boundaries. The virus threatens to cross over that border between Other and Self: the threat it poses is not only one of disease but one of dissolution, the contamination of categories."[19]

Attempts by the media to control the ensuing panic have resulted in an "epidemic of signification" about HIV and AIDS. Johnson's revelations sent media reportage into its greatest spiral on the subject—259 stories in the U.S. press the week of his announcement. The association between virus or syndrome and athlete is particularly problematic, because sporting prowess is derived from symbolic and physical transcendence. In the case of Magic Johnson, the virus was apparently transmitted as a result of the heterosexual male promiscuity that is conventional in elite American sporting culture. The "shock" of the announcement expressed in banner headlines was quickly followed by speculation about the future of Johnson's contracts to endorse corporate products and the possibilities of infection on the basketball court.[20] The interpenetration of capital and the body thus produced simultaneous panics of capital accumulation, viral contagion, and gendered and racialized sexuality—for at the moment of his announcement, African American men made up 6 percent of the U.S. population but accounted for 23 percent of its reported cases of AIDS.[21]

In media narratives, Johnson's disclosure of his HIV-positive status was framed within pre-existing channels of homophobia and misogyny. For instance, a pervasive theme was his unselfish "accommodation" of the female groupies who allegedly preyed on him.[22] In a *Sports Illustrated* article co-written with the journalist Roy Johnson, Magic stated that he was certain he had been infected by a woman who carried the virus but could not specify the time or place, because it was "a matter of numbers." After arriving in Los Angeles in 1979, he continued, "I did my best to accommodate as many women as I could—most of them through unprotected sex." He then pleaded with other athletes and entertainers who had been "out there" to get tested and practice safe sex, the clear assumption being that promiscuous male celebrities were *recipients* rather than *transmitters* of the virus, the origin of which was traced to insatiable women's desire. "It doesn't matter how beautiful the woman might be or how tempting she might sound on the telephone," Johnson said. "I know that we are pursued by women so much that it is easy to be weak. Maybe by getting the virus I'll make it easier for you guys to be strong."[23]

The male athlete as a victim of female predators also emerged in coverage of other basketball players and sports. A syndicated report from the *New York Times* entitled "Hockey Teams' Bad Dreams" opened with the statement: "Across Canada yesterday, players, coaches and fans of professional ice hockey anxiously struggled to come to terms with the disclosure by two Montreal doctors that a young woman who died of AIDS two years ago contended she had sex with 30 to 70 National Hockey League players."[24]

In the issue of *Sports Illustrated* in which Johnson made his disclosures, E. M. Swift described the "Dangerous Games" that male athletes played, including one NBA player "who estimates that he has slept with 2,500 different women, and counting." An article in *Time*, entitled "The Dangerous World of Wannabes," stated that "Magic Johnson's plight brings fear into the locker rooms across the U.S. and spotlights the riskiest athletic perk: promiscuous sex," a hazard graphically if improbably illustrated by "Hall of Famer Wilt Chamberlain [who] boasts of having slept with 20,000 women—an average of 1.4 a day for 40 years." Although two NBA players were quoted as saying that athletes had to take responsibility for their sexual behavior, a considerable portion of the text and graphics concentrated on the "Annies," "buckle bun-nies," and "wannabes" who allegedly "beguiled" baseball play-ers, rodeo riders, and other male athletes. A few years later, Cham-berlain died, alone and very suddenly. The 1991 boast (in his book *A View from Above*) was said to have lost him millions of dol-lars in endorsements. And he passed away shortly after admitting that it had been closer to 10,000 one-night stands after all.[25]

The crisis of the sexualized body is presented here as the inno-cently virile male besieged by "fatal attractors." This is not a wholly novel phenomenon: Images of women as "gold-diggers" and femmes fatales are familiar, as we saw with reference to NFL shibboleths, while "venereal diseases have typically been assigned a female identity." The idea of a global virus carried by sexually aggressive women and infecting reluctant, passive men gives a new twist to traditional sexual stigmatization. In Magic Johnson's case, it overrides conventional white men's fantasy fears about black men's sexual potency by writing sexual difference over racial difference. And racial indifference was long a part of Johnson's blinding mystique as an ideal citizen. As he put it in describing his rivalry with fellow NBA player Larry Bird: "It's hard to look at a white man and see black, but when I looked at Larry, that's what I saw." Magic Johnson is routinely described as open and friendly with the press—"the embodiment of Showtime with his million-dollar smile." He also epitomizes the fastidious patriarchal obeisance that middle-American culture celebrates: "After God and my father, I respect Larry Bird more than anyone."[26]

Male sports reporters demonstrated little professional skepti-cism about the assumptions that Magic Johnson's infection had come from packs of sexually marauding women. There was virtu-ally no concern for the women who had been in sexual contact with Johnson (apart from his wife, Cookie, with whom he had a socially sanctioned liaison). Journalists articulated the body panic sur-rounding HIV and AIDS and sports in ways that framed hetero-sexual women as virulent agents and heterosexual men as innocent victims. Such accounts are embedded in a gender order that privileges straight men's promiscuity and devalues, pathologizes, or criminalizes other forms of sexuality. Thus, the compassion and admiration initially expressed by journalists emerged not simply because Magic was a venerated athlete who became a "chance" victim of HIV infection, but also because he was a (hetero)sexual athlete. The possibility that Magic—or any other sportsman—could have had sex with other men was unacceptable at the time, although there were some implications in the *bourgeois* press, and rumors circulating in gay groups and on the basketball circuit that he had many boyfriends were finally repeated in mainstream newspapers in 1996.[27]

Overwhelmingly favorable media treatment of Magic Johnson (which would have been unlikely if he had confessed to homosexual or drug-use transmission or had presented a queer public persona like Rodman's) enabled him to come out of retirement to play on the "Dream Team" that won the gold medal at the 1992 Summer Olympics, then to return to the NBA, to public acclaim. Johnson's decision to play in the Olympics precipitated unease when some Australian athletes indicated that they were afraid of being infected by him and might not compete against the United States if he played. The resultant nationalist outburst put the body panic temporarily into reverse. Some American players and journalists responded with outrage and warned that they would hand Australia a severe defeat if the two teams met at the Games. Hundreds of protesting phone calls and some bomb threats were made to Australia's diplomatic missions in the United States. Australia's minister for foreign affairs publicly rebuked the team's medical director, who had recommended that players not compete against Magic.

In November 1992, Johnson again retired when some local opponents (including Karl Malone, one of his Olympic teammates and a National Rifle Association hunting advocate) expressed concern about being infected when Magic bled slightly following vigorous body contact during a pre-season game. It seemed as though

even Johnson, one of the most revered idols in the American sporting pantheon, could not overcome the AIDS panic and remain a
professional basketball player, instead devoting himself to education campaigns for safe sex (including a booklet "Safer Sex: What
You Can Do to Avoid AIDS") and higher levels of funding for
research. A *New York Times* journalist described Johnson as "our
greatest celebrity leper." In the ensuing period, Magic returned as
a player, retired again, then coached and toured with his all-star
team, on one occasion being refused entry into a country because
of his "medical condition." Today, he is held up as a paragon of
new black business virtue in his role as a cinema–theater entre-
preneur, and the Magic Johnson Foundation has donated more
than $10 million to communities dealing with HIV.[28]

Media narratives of the HIV and AIDS body panic in sports
were, in this instance, anchored by archetypes of male "super-
studs" and female "supergroupies." Sportsmen engaging in myriad one-night stands were depicted as at risk because they "accom-
modated" licentious women. In a classic scenario of sin and
redemption, women were framed as the cause of the HIV and
AIDS problem, and men were absolved of responsibility for their
actions.[29] In the case of Magic Johnson, it seems, the particular version of black maleness he represented deflected a racialized discourse of power toward gender. Symbolic violence was visited on
the sportsman through consensual sex with a stigmatized other—
the promiscuous woman (also often presented in media accounts
as predominantly black or Hispanic). The Magic affair, therefore,
can be distinguished from, yet has parallels with, another scandal
involving a sports star, first as rapist, then as "cannibal."

The Fall and Fall of "Iron" Mike

A. J. Ayer was at a party in New York, given by Fernando Sanchez, an ultra-
fashionable underwear designer, when a woman rushed in to report that her friend
was being assaulted in another room. Abandoning the young models, with whom

he was no doubt enjoying a philosophical discussion about logical positivism and the significance of the thong, Ayer went to investigate, finding an aroused Mike Tyson forcing himself on a distraught Naomi Campbell. Ayer warned Tyson to desist. Tyson retorted: "Do you know who the fuck I am? I'm the heavyweight champion of the world." Ayer stood fast and replied: "I am the former Wykeham Professor of Logic. We are both pre-eminent in our field; I suggest we talk about this like rational men." —Colin McGinn (1999)

In 1992, Florida police investigated a woman's charge that three New York Mets baseball players had raped her, and later in the year, former heavyweight champion Mike Tyson was convicted of rape. Commenting on these incidents, as well as on Magic Johnson, Wilt Chamberlain, the rape trial of William Kennedy Smith, and U.S. Senate Judiciary Committee hearings on charges of sexual harassment against Clarence Thomas, the reporter John Durie wrote:

> Baseball players . . . are notorious for accepting the advances of the groupies who mob them in team hotels after the game. The baseball season starts this month and, with spring training in Florida, this is the first chance for the groupies to make friends with a baseballer. It is not the last chance because the six-month season often splits players from their families. Players felt they were being victimized because they were rich, said Mr. Jesse Barfield, a Yankees outfielder. He noted that, "after this Tyson thing we have to be careful, we are easy targets."[30]

Once Tyson was sentenced, male reporters and lawyers began raising concerns about the fairness of the trial. African American ministers in Indiana circulated petitions saying that Tyson should be given a suspended sentence because of his heroic status. The Harvard law professor Alan Dershowitz launched an appeal, invoking themes that were strikingly similar to the Magic Johnson case. Russell Miller, for example, described Dershowitz (the successful attorney depicted in the Hollywood film *Reversal of Fortune* [1990] and later a member of O. J. Simpson's "dream team" of defense lawyers) as "a fearless champion of civil liberties" who had earned the enmity of "radical feminists" for claiming that rape should be categorized into degrees of criminality.

Miller went on to question the credibility of the plaintiff, Desiree Washington, and the jury, alleging that Tyson could not have received a fair trial because "events had conspired significantly against him" in the wake of the publicity surrounding Kennedy Smith and Thomas. Finally, Miller questioned the motive for the victim's legal action: "Was it because she had been raped, or was it because she had been treated like a cheap groupie?"[31] He quoted Dershowitz's contention that Washington took legal action because she was affronted by Tyson's suggestion that she either walk or take a limousine home after consenting to sexual intercourse: "This woman came on as a groupie. Everybody knows what the rules are for groupies who hang around famous athletes and rock stars. They get 15 or 20 minutes of not very good sex, no kiss goodnight, no telephone number, no appreciation. All they get are bragging rights—'I slept with the champ.'"

Washington, not Tyson, is positioned as guilty and aggressive. Miller notes that Dershowitz and one of Tyson's associates find him "sweet, soft-spoken and intelligent . . . a very bright guy." Like Magic Johnson, Tyson is portrayed as a victim of women's rapaciousness, who "is not finding it easy in jail. He is terrified of being set up, having drugs planted on him or getting into a fight by someone wanting to make a name for himself. . . . 'He is a man in a lot of pain,' says Dershowitz. . . . 'He doesn't understand why she did this to him. He understands that she might have been upset, but that's no excuse for destroying a man's life and career.'"

In this way, the body of Tyson is repositioned to acquire characteristics of feminine vulnerability from the now implicitly masculinized bodies of those women who take the sexual initiative, reversing the direction of "normal" corporeal power. The functional connection between the basketball groupie who infected Magic Johnson and the boxing groupie who undid "Iron" Mike Tyson is made clear in such statements: We are back to Benedict's shibboleths. Causality and culpability are carefully attributed within a gendered discourse that represents the valorized body of the elite male athlete (and, by extension, the male body per se) as devalued through hazardous exchange with the debased bodily currency of the sexually compromised female. This case, like the Thomas confirmation hearings, is further overdetermined by the competing affinities of gender and race.[32]

Tyson's defense, as per Magic Johnson's spin, drew on images of racialized and sexualized black sports masculinity, transmuting its symbolic invincibility into vulnerability by invoking another discourse of power—active women's sexuality. The body of the black male elite athlete is protected from racist discourses that seek to reduce it to no more than blind sexual urges—by projecting that identity onto the bodies of women. Such strategies are not always successful. Iron Mike did go to jail, but in less than half a decade he was back in the ring, having converted to Islam (as a matter of faith and a technology of the self). In June 1997, during a fight with Evander Holyfield, he bit off a portion of his opponent's lower earlobe, incurring widespread condemnation for "savagery." This assault sealed Tyson's fate as incapable of control both in and outside the ring, leaving him open to traditional white racist distrust of black male bodies. The Nevada Athletic Commission revoked Tyson's license to box until 1999, when he again returned to fighting until he was arrested for assaulting motorists, which also violated the conditions of his probation for the rape charge. He was imprisoned but released early on good behavior in the summer of 1999 and was free to fight again. This time, the bout was ended because his opponent suffered a severe injury when Tyson illegally hit him after the bell and he slipped to the canvas. The next return to the ring was marked by revived controversy over sexual violence, as women's groups sought to have Tyson barred from the United Kingdom for a 2000 bout because of his rape conviction.[33]

As in the Simpson trials, there are troubling and competing explanations here, according to the invocation of either gendered or racial discourses. Tyson is reported as saying, "I like to hurt women when I make love to them. I like to hear them scream and see them bleed. It gives me pleasure." His defense's rebuttal of the rape charge made much of the great difficulty he had in relating to women in a "normal" way. Yet, as John Sloop argues, the routine portrayal of Tyson as a "man-beast-machine," and a corresponding differentiation of Desiree Washington from negative images of black women, produced a highly racialized prima facie supposition of Tyson's guilt:

> Playing into the myths of the black man and the black athlete, it becomes only logical that Tyson is guilty. Again, the crime is seen as all the more unforgivable once we consider the repositioning of Desiree Washington as something other than the stereotypical black. Washington, given the subject position of the college student and Sunday-school teacher, is able effectively to shed the myths of the stereotype of the promiscuous African American woman and allowed to become the sexually naive and innocent debutante, whitened to such a degree that Tyson's inevitable rape is both more predictable and all the more unforgiveable.[34]

The difficulty of disentangling assumptions of guilt and innocence from pre-existing racist and sexist discourses—not to mention the knowing exploitation of those discourses by both prosecution and defense—reveals the extent to which ideologies of power are ever-present in the practice of everyday life and the conduct of cultural politics.[35]

Rodman's excesses and the Ben Johnson, Magic Johnson, and Mike Tyson affairs invoke myths of the black man's inherent physical advantage, translated into white conceptions (and fears) of sporting and sexual prowess.[36] The image of the black male sporting body, like that of the black male pop star, is heavily sexualized. There is no absolute correspondence here between mythos and interpretation, of course. For example, in the case of Arthur Ashe, primary reference was to his medical acquisition of HIV and AIDS. Nevertheless, the generally idealized sexual capacity of the black man readily reinforces the symbolic potency of these narratives. Even the most heroically

formidable embodiments of heterosexual masculinity are overcome by a sexualized, feminized disorder.

The mythic downfall of the "black superstud"[37] can also be
placed in the service of a full-blown, multifaceted body panic. In
a facetious attack on the control and mooted banning of sports
sponsorship by the tobacco industry, for instance, Jeff Wells
invents a letter from a David D. (presumably standing for
Klan/Republican politician David Duke) of Louisiana to an Australian named Fred. Wells's article, couched in the language of bigotry, represents athletes' bodies as subject to fascist control:

> See the links? Smoking-sport-in-the-dark-races-sex-AIDS-fags?
> I tell you, when I read that book of Roland Fishman's you sent
> me, and then heard about Magic Johnson, I wished I was back
> with the Klan.
>
> So the Australian cricketers went off to the West Indies and
> Fishman tells us that there was so much skirt chasing going on
> that it was no wonder that your boys couldn't perform during the
> day.
>
> And are we supposed to believe that it was only the white
> ladies your boys were fooling around with?
>
> Then Magic Johnson announces that he has AIDS. And that he
> got it from a woman. And he sure hasn't been ignoring those
> black mommas all these years.
>
> If Magic Johnson has AIDS then who knows what is going on
> in cricket? Or the Olympics, where the athletes of all colours
> don't seem to be able to keep their hands off each other. Ban
> sport Fred![38]

Wells's rhetoric animates "panic sport," as the control of tobacco
promotion masks an agenda to ban sports and suppress polymorphous pleasure. This, however, is not an instance of playful post-
modernist irony, but a right-wing populist exploitation of the con-
notative linkages between sports and diverse physical practices.
In this instance, the sexuality of Magic Johnson (and, in a more
diffuse way, the Australian men's cricket team) is used to sym-
bolize corporeal freedom. Racialized sports sexuality can be
placed in the service of many discourses, but they are rarely pro-

gressive, and they absolve the implied guilt of one subordinate group by transferring it to another.

It is clear that the figure of the black sporting man retains its positive and negative valences. Contested images of black sportsmen continue to emerge, occupying vast politico-cultural space. On the negative side, the Simpson trials, for example, afforded an extended opportunity for the interrogation of the black male sports body on and off the field of play.[39] More positively, Jordan's ubiquitous image posits highly attractive signs of black masculinity in the entertainment media against extremely negative meanings in the news media.

What Is to Be Done?

Readers will be familiar with the black man as a target of critical mavens in search of guilt and blame for social ills that can be displaced onto either the media or individuals from the systematic inequality and brutality of capitalism, sexism, and racism. Whereas team sports were valorized for their functionalist effects by Spiro Agnew and the Durkheimians, here they are vilified from an equally conservative position. Sports turn from an appropriate outlet for biologically determined violent tendencies into an uncontrolled source of machismo.

There are, of course, counters to violence and sports that problematize psychologistic and commercial answers, looking instead at the climate of systematic, institutional violence done by capitalism and the state. In the United States, this political-economy-of-culture approach keys us to the realization that sports are used to pacify and metaphorize on behalf of accumulation and governance. A surrogate group is selected for sacrificial violence. Social tensions are projected onto this group in order to bind a social formation that lacks a properly legitimized juridical apparatus[40] (as per the dysfunctional democracy of the United States, where the vast majority of citizens believe there is no value in voting).

If we link this to the data on scarcity, it becomes clear that the disparity between the imaginary and the symbolic in the public circulation of black masculinity is central. Young African American men suffer almost 60 percent unemployment and high levels of homelessness, illness, and incarceration. Homicide is the principal cause of death for black males age eighteen to twenty-nine, and men make up only 20 percent of African American college graduates.[41] Black men are poster boys for a scarcity that is slotted home by the biases of marginalist economics to personal qualities and pathologized by welfarists and God-botherers as outcomes of the "decline" in heteronormative family arrangements. But within this cohort, young African American athletes in the three most lucrative U.S. professional sports (baseball, basketball, and football) have extremely high incomes and low levels of the indices cited earlier. Yet some are not the well-disciplined utility maximizers and heads of household so beloved of both Daniel Patrick Moynihan and Louis Farrakhan. *These* young black men are poster boys for the value placed by audiences on popular culture, even though they come from the most comprehensively demonized group in American public life. In short, the scarcity ethos of American capitalism blames impoverished black youth for financial "failure" and blames popular culture for wealthy black youth's financial "success": When they lose, it's because of personal idiosyncracies; when they win, it's because of social decadence.

This is not to deny the salience of men's sexual violence and its connection to sports. Some explain rape by black men as a politicized response to their collective situation—an indefensible throwback to the logic of Eldridge Cleaver. But the high level of suspicion and investigation of African American men in public space is more relevant, and this surveillance inevitably generates bad numbers, given the universality of men's violence against women. When linked to claims for a "genetic basis to criminality" through the obsessive analysis of black men in prisons—and through George Bush the Elder's "Violence Prevention Initiative," which sought to "screen" 100,000 inner-city children "to identify potential criminals"—it's pretty clear that we're witnessing the displacement onto surrogate victims of the downside to scarcity. Such scapegoating distracts attention from the fact that scarcity is crucial for capitalism: Charging rent for the occupancy of space and the consumption of goods is ineffective without the threat of penury. Across the 1990s, the retreats from welfare initiatives born during Lyndon Johnson's administration put poverty exactly where it was before civil-rights legislation was enacted: White workers form a high percentage of the poor, with Latinos and Latinas and African Americans represented out of all proportion to their slice of the population.[42] This return to Eisenhower has been achieved through macroeconomic adjustment, divide-and-rule racist assaults on "poverty solidarity," and the psychologization and pathologization of black men, in particular.

Again, we see evidence of counter-power. Consider the film *Jerry Maguire* (1997), in which stereotypes of black and white American masculinity crisscross in fascinating ways. A white sports agent (played by Tom Cruise) is publicly stricken with guilt at the exploitative operation of his business—not the principle of it, but the hypocrisy of preaching care and attention to athletes when one has too many on the roster. And he feels the need to "share" this with colleagues. But that is not the main lesson of the film. Following Cruise's blinding conversion to the confessional, he gets the sack. The one client who remains with him is a black football player (played by Cuba Gooding, Jr.). Gooding's problem is that he has attitude: toward his teammates, his coaches, and the media. He is an overt utilitarian who wants material recognition for his efforts as a professional but refuses to look as though he cares about his sport or his club. At home, by comparison, he is a caring, loving husband and father whose passions help to drive a functioning and happy family.

This is not a depiction of the African American sportsman or parent that gets much currency in the white *bourgeois* media.

Appreciating the domestic harmony on view, Cruise himself marries but cannot bring his brand-new discourse of feelings to bear on his home life. The two men meet and address their dilemmas by confronting each other. In a great moment of rearticulation, the black man is told to put more of his love and passion into public display, to blend the private with the public, while the white man is told to transfer the "I love you" side of his profession to home—quite a reversal of the homilies normally read to African Americans by policymakers. But the film does not overtly account for these transferences and counter-transferences in racial terms. Instead, we are diminished by its return to narratives of interiority and psychic completeness, in classical Hollywood fashion—but at least we have seen an alternative representation along the way, a welcome addition and corrective to the stereotypes evident in this chapter.

Each time we are encouraged to associate the mad and the immoral with black youth, we should turn our attention to systematic violence done by the state and business through: 1) the structural conditions erected by elites such as college presidents and sports-franchise owners; 2) environmental despoliation; and 3) violence to the safe passage, free talk, and public-sphere occupancy of women and minorities. Maybe NFL rookie orienteers (the teachers, not the pupils) could take Feminism 1000 while they're at it. Stop rounding up the usual suspects; start dealing with the actual causes. Then we might reverse Spiro Agnew's interest in glue and Douglas MacArthur's fascination for seed in favor of Cuba Gooding, Jr.'s, plaintive cry: "Show me the money!"

4

Courting Lesbianism

with Jim McKay and Randy Martin

I looked like a butch lesbian. It was supposed to be spiky and Brad Pitt-y. But I looked like a female Wimbledon champion. —*Hugh Grant on a haircut (as quoted in "Hugh" 1999)*

After defeating world number-one Lindsay Davenport in the 1999 Australian Open Tennis semifinals, Amélie Mauresmo "leapt into the arms of girlfriend Sylvie Bourdon and was cradled with hugs." Throughout the match, Bourdon had been "pumping her fists and yelling, '*Allez!*' ['Go!']." Following a whirlwind romance, begun just a month or two earlier, they had moved in together and embarked on a joint workout regime of several hours of weightlifting each week. Now they were on tour.[1] Mauresmo came out to the media during the open. She was the first-ever French athlete to come out.[2]

Davenport had attained the world's top ranking by developing a style suited to her six feet, two inches of height and marked strength. She was defeated at her own game. Although five inches shorter, Mauresmo prevailed due to her superb physical condition, a fast and accurate serve, and a hard topspin forehand (traditionally used only by male players). Until Mauresmo's victory, the media had barely noticed her, even though she had been world junior champion in 1996. But after the post-match media conference, Mauresmo became front-page news, because Davenport said: "A couple of times, I mean, I thought I was playing a guy, the girl was hitting so hard, so strong. . . . [S]he is so strong in those shoulders and she just hits the ball very well. . . . I mean, she hits the ball not like any other girl. She hits it so hard and with so much topspin. . . . Women's tennis isn't usually played like that."

In addition to this tacit criticism (or, at least, othering) of her opponent for displaying "unnatural" power, Davenport also sparked speculation that Mauresmo may have attained her physique through drugs, commenting that her shoulders "looked huge to me. I think they must have grown; maybe because she's wearing a tank top." Mauresmo responded to Davenport thus: "The fact that I'm strong physically is maybe impressing her. It means that I'm a very solid player, so I take it as a compliment."[3]

Of course, Mauresmo's musculature is unexceptional next to that of such players as Mary Pierce and Venus and Serena Williams. This suggests that sexuality animated the controversy. Before their match to decide the Australian Open, Martina Hingis told reporters that Mauresmo "came to Melbourne with her girlfriend; I think she's half a man." Mauresmo exclaimed: "On top of wanting to beat her, now I'm enraged!" Hingis apologized and supposedly discussed the issue with Mauresmo following the final, but then advised *Sports Illustrated:* "I'm not regretting anything I said about her." Ironically named for the out lesbian Martina Navratilova, Hingis also told a press conference after the open that "it wouldn't be very healthy for all the girls to go through five sets" and referred to herself as "one of the Spice Girls of tennis." The founding mother of women's professional tennis, Billie Jean King, asked Chris Evert, Hingis's tour mentor, to counsel against this homophobic speech, and even Steffi Graf criticized it. The new joke ran: "What do you get when Rupert Murdoch meets

Martina Hingis? Tabloid heaven, essentially." Faced with critical French journalists in Paris, Hingis suggested that she and Mauresmo face off in Mike Tyson fashion: "Maybe we should meet in a boxing fight and bite each other's ears."[4]

The Australian sporting media went into a frenzy over Mauresmo's lesbianism and body. Melbourne's *Herald Sun* featured her in pictures from the rear, on court, and necking with Bourdon, under the headline, "Oh, Man, She's Good." Other headlines indicate the depth of press anxiety and sensationalism: "Bourdon works in a bistro near her St. Tropez home called Le Gorille. Translation: Gorilla. Just don't tell Lindsay Davenport" (*The Age*); "Women normally only play tennis against men in mixed doubles. But that all changed yesterday if you believe the world's number one player Lindsay Davenport" and "shoulders like Lou Ferrigno—she is the French 'incroyable hulk.' . . . Where is women's tennis headed? Mind boggles at the muscle monsters" (*Daily Telegraph*); "'Man' Taunts Fire Up Mauresmo . . . Mauresmo Out in the Open" (*Weekend Australian*); and "Grace v. Power: An Eternal Struggle" (*Sydney Morning Herald*).[5]

North American press comments on Mauresmo's body veered from surprise at "her strong chin and muscular shoulders" through comparison to "the best 200-meter butterfly swimmers in the world," "huge linebacker shoulders," and "the shoulders of an Olympic swimmer" to discriminating critiques of her femininity as "rather manly . . . a bit butch, with masculine facial features," culminating in the Reuters News Agency's query: "Who Is This Guy?"[6]

The controversy was handled quite differently by the commentators Fred Stolle, Patrick McEnroe, Cliff Drysdale, Pam Shriver, and Mary-Jo Fernandez of the U.S. sports cable network ESPN2, and by John Alexander of Australia's Channel 7 (coverage of 29 January 1999). Drysdale criticized the Australian media, describing Davenport's remarks as "much ado about nothing" and agreeing with Mauresmo that "to say that somebody plays like a man, I think that is a compliment." McEnroe applauded Mauresmo's handling of the situation, paraphrasing her: "I'm here with my girlfriend; what's the big deal?" Drysdale concurred, while Stolle stated matter-of-factly that "she lives with her girlfriend down in St. Tropez—spends time in the gym with her." In noting the emphasis on power in Mauresmo's game, McEnroe admiringly acknowledged a change—that this "may be the future of women's tennis." Shriver and Fernandez previewed the final without referring to the controversy, other than alluding to Mauresmo's supposedly masculine game. Alexander expressed admiration for Mauresmo's hard work, physical condition, and dedication. During the final, the cameras cut about equally among the play, Hingis's mother, and Mauresmo's girlfriend, but the last was verbally identified less often.

At her press conference after the match, Mauresmo talked about closeted players on the tour, saying that they "had a hard time dealing with their situation.... I feel sorry for them." She had decided before the tournament to come out, because she felt that her sexuality would be a topic of debate and it was best to clear the air. Shriver, president of the Women's Tennis Association (WTA), said, "If the commercial world embraces her, it's a different era," alluding to Navratilova's earlier history of sparse endorsements and sponsorships. Mauresmo said that she expected to maintain her clothing contract, and "if they want to set me aside, there will be dozens more who will take me.... And if they let me go for that, they are jerks anyway." Some months later, all of Mauresmo's sponsors had stayed loyal, and she was featured in the WTA's 2000 tour calendar.[7]

Meanwhile, record ratings were posted for Australian TV's coverage, and the WTA announced it was continuing with pre-tournament/pre-out plans to feature Mauresmo in a marketing campaign, even as fears were voiced about the association's search for a new sponsor. Mauresmo practiced on Melbourne courts with bodyguards, and French television satirists made a puppet with her head on Arnold Schwarzenegger's body, accompanied by the following voice-over: "It's the first time in the history of French sports that a man says he is a lesbian." French lesbian groups rallied behind her.[8]

Clearly, homophobia was at work in the inference that Mauresmo—and not Davenport, Pierce, or the Williams sisters—pushed the limits of tennis's transgenderization. A predicament faced the heteronormativity that so suffuses women's tennis today: Passing on court as women's champion disrupted what women were being asked to pass as off the court. This gender play in turn cast the putative maleness of the men's game into doubt, on which more later. What was the background to this inflection of Sportsex?

The Sporting Body

One is physically fit when (1) she is free from disease, (2) does not have significant deviations from normal body structure or function, (3) has sufficient strength, speed, agility, endurance, and skill to do the maximum tasks of daily life, (4) is mentally and emotionally adjusted, and (5) has high moral and spiritual concepts.
—M. Vannier and H. B. Poindexter (1960, 4)

What do Margaret Smith Court, Renee Richards, Billie Jean King, Martina Navratilova, and Amélie Mauresemo have in common? They are all elite female tennis players who became the focus of moral panic in the popular media for "playing like a man." The latter four were framed as doubly abject—Richards for being a transsexual, and King, Navratilova, and Mauresmo for being lesbians (very openly in the last two cases). The U.S. Tennis Association and the WTA disaffiliated some events in which Richards competed, and these tournaments were also boycotted by many players, while the WTA has routinely tried to downplay same-sex affinities among players. For their part, journalists used the controversies to construct and normalize gender, sex, and sexuality.[9]

By contrast, Evert, the ur-"white American darling" (a mode of embodiment rather than simply a style of play; we'll abbreviate it as WAD) was portrayed as the ethical and textual center of tennis, her choice of makeup and earrings calculated to attract sponsors and spectators and her "cool and delicate-looking" style deemed more demure than that of stronger-looking players. She became notorious for proclaiming, "I don't think any point is worth falling down for" (later recast as an ironized comment about technical superiority, not politesse). Two years after she retired, when Navratilova was still playing, Evert was the country's most popular tennis celebrity and Navratilova ranked number 27. When the latter was honored at a fund-raiser for the 1994 Gay Games, U.S. newspapers gave the event almost no coverage.[10]

Everyday discursive practices invariably construct "women who become like men" as deviants. The emphasis in sports on intimidation, violence, and physical prowess, as well as on sports' misogynistic, homophobic, and male homosocial valences, mean that sportswomen who challenge gender norms usually face formidable resistance. Nevertheless, as noted earlier, traditional athletic ideologies of masculine superiority have been destabilized as women have gained greater access to sport. Yet their presence also poses threats to masculinity, precipitating male "hysteria" and attempts by men to contain women's aspirations and resistance. It also produces a cosmic ambivalence when women actually compete with men's physiques—recall the sequence in the movie *A League of Their Own* (1992) when Marla, a stupendous home-run hitter who is "masculine looking," undergoes a makeover and is resumed to heterosexuality through marriage.[11]

Women's bodybuilding has gone through major shifts over the past fifteen years that show these discourses at work. The film *Pumping Iron II: The Women* (1985) finds the 1983 Women's World Cup at Caesar's Palace thrown into confusion by the power lifter Bev Francis, who juxtaposes her own refusal to "go out there trying to cocktease" with accusations that she is "an overmuscular woman." At a judges' meeting prior to the event, convened to deal with this new body shape, the chair explains their task to his colleagues:

We hope that this evening we can clear up the definite meaning, the analysis of the word "femininity" and what you have to look for. . . . [W]e're looking for something that's right down the middle. A woman that has a certain amount of aesthetic femininity but yet has that muscle tone to show that she's an athlete. . . . Women are women and men are men and there's a difference, and thank God for that difference. . . . We don't want to turn people on . . . uh, off . . . we want to turn them on.

Francis finished eighth in the field. Four years later, she won the Women's World Championship and placed high in Ms. Olympia from 1987 to 1991. Just as the judges changed in their views of her somatotype, so Francis changed, via cosmetic surgery, hair dye, and pink bikinis. Bodybuilding has developed to the point at which men and women preparing for competition enter what the ethnographer, judge, and participant Anne Bolin sees as a state of "liminality and antistructure" that problematizes gender binaries even as it heightens tensions over the relationship between muscularity and sex. Women are now expected to be a bizarre amalgam of muscular and feminine, complying with both anti-norms and hyper-norms of femininity, a sculpted self-presentation in the name of liberation that blends "big" hair and steroid abuse. The positive and negative sides to this were endorsed as art in the exhibit "Picturing the Modern Amazon" at Manhattan's New Museum of Contemporary Art in 2000.[12]

Even the "acceptable" female athlete has her body scrutinized. Hingis's relative failure in 1998 (one Grand Slam victory and the eventual loss of her number-one ranking after a miraculous first year on the senior circuit) was attributed by *Sports Illustrated* to "the physical and emotional effects of just growing up," as her body "became wider and softer, hampering her coordination."[13]

The "feminization of women's tennis," as King called it, became part of the professional game's business strategy in the 1980s. It was quickly picked up by the media, via sexualization of the female sporting body in a manner akin to soft-core-porn advertising, with the predominantly passive female athlete functioning as the object of the male gaze. This is particularly prominent in the annual swimsuit issue of *Sports Illustrated*, the *Golden Girls of Athletics* and *Golden Girls of Sport* calendars, and *Inside Sport* and *Sports Monthly* magazines. It is based on the antithesis men's sport:women's bodies.[14] We sense that events such as the Mauresmo affair put that bifurcation at risk—or, at least, signify its instability.

Writing Tennis/Writing Lesbianism

"This is the best part of all, taking a picture with the trophy, in a social dress," Hingis said, flipping her freshly sprayed bob and smiling wickedly through layers of makeup applied for the occasion. Abruptly she unzipped her suede jacket, revealing the spectacular red minidress she hadn't worn in September. "This is quite cute, I think," she said. "Don't you?" —*Tim Layden (1999b)*

When tennis arrived in the United States in the 1870s, it was seen as not overly vigorous—in fact, it was a suitable candidate for putting ruling-class daughters on display to single men. Within a decade, the white *bourgeois* country-club world of the U.S. Lawn Tennis Association was in play. Women engaged in international competition from 1900, via the Wightman Cup, and today they make up 58 percent of registered U.S. players.[15]

The "question" of femininity has always been central to women's tennis, from medical to media discourse and back. In the late nineteenth century, gynecology debated whether women should play tennis during menstruation, and biologically derived excuses for restricting women's participation in sports have continued. Medical articles and educational manuals on the relevance of sports to young women were more overtly ideological in discouraging activities coded as masculine. During the inter-World War period, the American Medical Association worried that basketball could impede "the organic vitality of a growing girl," placing undue strain on the uterus during menstruation. Into the 1940s, tennis was deemed risky because it was thought to promote over-development of abdominal muscles, which might hinder child-birth.[16] The corollary was that competing without regard to one's cycle was somehow to be less a woman. There have been homologies in the association of styles of play with genders—by the 1960s, men were instructed to use power via a serve-and-volley game or vicious topspin, while women should emphasize grace and finesse.

Occasionally, female players have forged an alchemical miracle of "man-like strokes" and "feminine grace," exemplified in the success of Helen Wills across the Depression. Wills became the first WAD of the court. In the '20s, the dominant player had been Suzanne Lenglen, a "flapper"-like figure who sipped alcohol between games, moved like a dancer, wore short skirts, and declined to marry. She was known as the "best-loved young nymph" of the sport—a fusion of unavailability and femininity that served to beguile and made her an international celebrity. Wills's demureness, girlish demeanor, and class signifiers gave her a traditional, "moral" appeal, by contrast to Lenglen, but both players were testimony to middle-class women resisting seclusion from the public world. Wills's nickname of "Little Miss Poker Face" evidenced the steely, efficient side of WADism, while Alice Marble, next to dominate the scene, had a power game that intimidated many men.[17]

Despite gynecological panics, by the 1940s, tennis was an ordinary component of physical education for middle-class white women. Instructional manuals emphasized the need for certain native qualities—"good rhythm, balance, footwork, and power"—which could be supplemented by training. A fast and well-placed serve was proposed, along with attacking net play, and a "dress or shorts" was recommended, with the rule of thumb "freedom of movement."[18] No sense of any prohibition here on strength or comfort. Manuals from the following decades were similarly technical and gender-neutral in their instruction.

But the psy-complexes (psychology, psychoanalysis, and psychiatry) eventually turned up for work, socializing students into

notions of the greater collective good and gender roles and allay-
ing fears of lesbianism-through-tennis. During the 1950s, psy-
chologists maintained that "normal" sexual development was at
risk through gender segregation in sports. This concern arose as
part of Cold War cultural normalization. Female athletes were
under notice to assert their heterosexuality, and "mannishness"
became a negative trope of sports journalism. For women, associations were drawn between spinsterhood and sporting activity;
men, by contrast, were thought less likely to be gay if they played
sports when young. So female students of physical education were
given special lessons in attracting men, required to shave their
legs, and instructed in appropriate hairdos, while athletics officials
promulgated statistics emphasizing the high levels of young athletes who went on to marry. This drew a riposte from many "out"
butch athletes, who specialized in duck-ass hair cuts, men's
footwear, and so on.[19]

Given tennis's colonial origin, it is relevant to note the landmark
achievements of Althea Gibson, the sport's first leading African
American. Gibson was the best player in the world in the late
1950s, with "explosive power" her stock in trade. Gibson's
social/racial distance from the polite, exclusionary norms of the
court touches on a profound truth about tennis and its cross-gender politics—what King called "a perfect combination of a violent
action taking place in an atmosphere of total tranquility . . . almost
like having an orgasm."[20]

Today's pro players owe a debt to the women's movement,
which re-emerged alongside the tennis rage of the 1970s. King's
activism not only advocated but was propelled by the burgeoning presence of women in the workforce. For many viewers, she
represented a class as well as a gender revolution, dragging tennis from its upper-crust origins to the rock era, and she was the
first American woman to learn the (mostly male) Australian model
of "percentage tennis," a form of risk-averse play that imported
rational calculation from economics to sport.[21] Feminism's social

agonism had its tennis equivalent in the match arranged between King and the former Wimbledon champion and latter-day hustler Bobby Riggs.

Despite this link to feminist politics, when women's tennis developed from country-club amateurism to professional tournament play in the early 1970s, a great deal of effort went into maintaining the sport's genteel image, with the WTA refusing sponsorships from manufacturers of "feminine hygiene" products. The private and public worlds of the women's game underwent major shifts that encouraged disclosure/construction of a self away from the court. Starting in 1985, the WTA published a calendar, with leading players attired in evening gowns or bathing suits. It also invited them to talk about their private lives—a simultaneously humanizing and commodifying device. The negative side to this development is represented by Rita Mae Brown's criticism that the women's tour, perceived in the early '70s as a "feminist epiphany," had turned into a site where "players are packaged and marketed if not as latter-day Shirley Temples, then as retro-women."[22]

For all this attention to the personal, television cameras rarely focused on Navratilova's girlfriends during matches, and Wimbledon announcers always referred to her as "Miss." For with the increasing commodification of women's sport has come a new wave of "dyke-bashing." As noted earlier, Avon, long a strong supporter of women's tennis, ceased its sponsorship in 1981 in the wake of King's "galimony" suit and Navratilova's relationship with Rita Mae Brown (which Navratilova denied at first because it put her application for U.S. citizenship at risk, when headlines dubbed her "the bisexual defector"). This closeting led to an unflattering depiction of the player in Brown's *roman à clef, Sudden Death*, one of a stream of lesbian sports novels that records a highly competitive world.[23]

In 1990, Margaret Smith Court, an Australian champion of the 1960s who had suffered from taunts about her femininity and had gone on to marry into a plutocratic Christian family, held a press conference at which she alerted the media that women's pro tennis was full of predatory lesbians who seduced young women into their ways—a "group of lesbian–bisexual players on the circuit, and they're the ones who get at the youngsters." Then Gabriela Sabatini said, "I don't even like to take my clothes off in the dressing room," and was joined in her moral panic by Graf, Jennifer Capriati, and Monica Seles, while Hana Mandlikova said that Navratilova "must have a chromosomic screw loose somewhere," and Alexandra Stevenson's mother announced at the 1999 Wimbledon that the tour was a hotbed of lesbian sedition and bizarre initiation rites. (Mandlikova's derision is odd, given her reported civil ceremony with Jana Novotna in 1990.[24])

All of this became front-page news in the *National Enquirer.* Against that, Navratilova usefully problematized lesbian panic in one of her tennis detective novels, as has the noted crime-fiction writer Sara Paretsky. Lucy Jane Bledsoe's account of lesbian panic on a college basketball team is equally moving.[25]

The controversy erupted toward the end of Navratilova's preeminence in tennis, which had long seen derision of her "lifestyle" by reference not only to her choice of sexual object but to certain signifiers of power: She was said to have "developed 'unnatural,' 'masculine' strength through weight training." These signifiers created the controversy as much as anything else, since the data about sex between established and young sportspeople reveal a pattern of senior men having sex with young men and women, not of senior and junior women conjugating. At the same time, the old gay rallying cry ("Think we're disgusting? Damn right we are"), which seeks to turn negative stereotypes into positive attributes, has also been claimed for lesbians and sports. Confronted with the need to sanitize and deny, some activists and scholars are now arguing for sports as a powerful source of and site for lesbian community, effectively rejecting a liberal politics that says, "Don't worry; we'll leave your daughters alone," in favor of a more radical claim that "lesbian existence *should* be feared." So when Donna Lopiano, executive director of the Women's Sport

Foundation, attacks the implication that "women who play sports or those who play at a particular school are lesbians" as "unethical," she is buying into the conventional liberal logic that says lesbians are acceptable but non-normative. Her position is tolerant, yes, but it also accepts that lesbianism is far from a universal virtue—it remains something to be "accused of." The foundation has a long history of anxiety on this topic. It is a tragic irony that U.S. colleges, where so much "passionate, open, and radical gay organizing is going on," and where there is such a strong history of lesbian athletes and coaches, find the latter as deeply oppressed and closeted as ever—a sign of the distance still to be traveled between cultural politics and American sports—while the friendly feelings of lesbians toward sports have even been challenged as part of American exceptionalism by scholars from elsewhere.[26]

Playing innocent about these matters from the mythos of liberalism is unworthy. When the Olympic gold medallist Dot Richardson became a U.S. icon after the Atlanta Games, she published an article in *Sports Illustrated*'s offshoot *Women/Sport* denying rumors that she was a lesbian and depicting her boyfriend. Associated moral panics about heterosexual womanhood being claimed for lesbianism leave many athletes "closeted" for "fear of losing scholarships [and] sponsorships," while women's sports-advocacy entities have had to deny lesbianism at every turn. In 1997, the basketball star Rebecca Lobo's TV commercial for Reebok reassured viewers/consumers that "women can be athletes and still be feminine," the mother of Houston Comets phenomenon Sheryl Swoopes proudly asserted that she had left the University of Texas because the team included lesbians (a comment that helped to send that team to the bottom of national rankings), and the Women's National Basketball Association decisively projected heteronormativity in its promotions. As Pat Griffin says, femininity works here as "a code word for heterosexuality." After his defeat by an all-woman sailing crew in the 1995 America's Cup, San Diego *bourgeois* Dennis Connor dubbed the

Mighty Mary "that lesbo boat."[27] There is no end to the political humiliations visited on lesbians in sports by their opponents.

Susan Fox Rogers introduces her anthology of critical and fictional writings on lesbianism and sports with an account of her own coming out. Where was she supposed to *go*, once she had emerged? "My choices seemed to be the bar, or the softball field—the two loci of women's gatherings." This is the flip side to the *nostrum* that "women who play sports are mannish, and mannish women are lesbians." Sports *are* a place to look for sexual community, just as they are a site for sexual fantasy: Here is the body on display, asking for evaluation and projection, and sold as such. Consider published fantasies by women about Navratilova and her heroization as a role model for young queers. The upside to her visibility is as part of "lesbian chic," a consumerist–celebrity hybrid form that can turn marginality into market position, as per burgeoning lesbian sports tourism.[28]

Returning to tennis, it would not be so hard to make the case for convergence between men and women. Venus Williams serving at more than 120 miles per hour does not surpass Greg Rusedki's 148 mph record-breaker, but her serve is fast even for the men's game. The grunts of Seles that accompanied her ground-strokes were never called manly, and many female professional players now generate equivalent pace, with or without the sound effects. Conversely, men are producing elongated, strategic rallies long thought of as the hallmark of women's tennis.

The doubleness returns at the level of remuneration, but again, tennis provides some cracks in the patriarchal story. The Association of Tennis Professionals and the WTA are parallel corporations charged with distinguishing their product lines. While women at the top of the game can take home seven-figure winnings, outside the top twenty players in the world, their earnings are roughly half those of men, typically in the lower six figures. Of the four major Open events (the Australian, the French, Wimbledon, and the U.S.), the first three do not pay equal prize money to men and women. Still, women have perhaps come further toward parity in tennis than in other sports. In 1975, Evert earned more in tournament pay than Ashe (the men's number one) and the leading golfer Jack Nicklaus. But twenty years later, Graf was the only woman to appear in *Forbes* magazine's list of the wealthiest forty athletes.[29]

Women's tennis has been relatively free to elaborate its social and economic value on the basis of a stylistics of play and a star system that clearly beat the men on their own terrain. While Pete Sampras scrambled to equal Roy Emerson's record twelve Open titles, which stood for nearly three decades, Hingis at nineteen and with six such wins was on track to overtake thirty-year-old Graf's twenty-two Open crowns. Graf herself surpassed the nineteen titles amassed by Navratilova, who played until she was nearly forty and returned to pro doubles at forty-four. The lower half of the women's quarterfinal draw at the 1999 Australian Open included Hingis, Graf, and Seles (the latter unbeaten through four previous appearances at the tournament). Together, they had won the event ten times. On the men's side, the corollary numbers totaled zero. This concentration of talent has produced sustained rivalries of the sort that build cultural investment and audience.

In the strictest calculus of political economy, women's expanded labor time was generating more value. There was at least a basis for the price of their efforts to rise, as well. But as a commodity, the value of tennis has no such transparency. Like any other sport that has been professionalized, its value is mediated. The way in which women's tennis appears in public (as opposed to how it is played) reinscribes the sport into a more general sexual economy. Gender returns through this mediation, with a vengeance. And so we turn now to that process.

Media Tennis

The inference from the coverage of Mauresmo's story is that she is somehow a problem for women's tennis, that her lesbianism is an embarrassment and that her size and power somehow disrupts the marketing plan, which seems to be based around Anna Kournikova. —Sydney Morning Herald (as quoted in Dutter and Parsons 1999)

Sports Illustrated marked Chris Evert's retirement with a cover story entitled "Now I'm Going to Be a Full-Time Wife," refining this suburban mythography with a photo montage of her ex-lovers. A decade later, the sex part of that syntagm was increasingly important to the women's game. In the lead-up to the 1998 U.S. Open, Venus Williams, Anna Kournikova, and Martina Hingis each graced the cover of a major fashion magazine. This double duty as icons of the feminine is part of a conjuncture that goes well beyond tennis. A front-page spread in "Business Day" of the *New York Times* (Saturday, 30 January 1999, C1, C4) reports on the displacement of supermodels by "celebrities" as cover girls of record for women's representation. Oprah Winfrey (October 1998) out-*Vogue*d the model Carolyn Murphy (August 1998) by 810,000 copies to 520,000, and Courtney Love (October 1997) sold almost 100,000 more issues of *Bazaar* than did Linda Evangelista (March 1997), while Kournikova queried the magazine: "Why should I look ugly just because I'm an athlete" and listed her tastes in Prada, Versace, and Chloe. *Sports Illustrated* called the 1999 U.S. Open "a lost episode of *Sex and the City*."[30] It would be a stretch to see these celebrity women as typical of the female nine-to-fiver. But if the star of the supermodel is experiencing even a partial eclipse, it is interesting to speculate on whether the high-modern ideal of beauty for beauty's sake is on the wane. The imaginary of feminine beauty—or, more broadly, the mimetic ideal—is being rearticulated to women's bodies that do different work from the traditional. This opens up spaces of women's performativity and burdens the newly reborn women with yet another version of the double shift.

Of course, these articulations can be trivializing in the extreme. Consider the following descriptions of female competitors at the 1998 Australian Open:

- The striking blonde Russian Anna Kournikova, tipped by some pundits to be the game's next superstar, is not your average adolescent.... Her stunning appearance and obvious talent combine to drive a million-dollar business.
- For sex, read the preening Mary Pierce, the pubescent Nabokovian Anna Kournikova. Perhaps the petite South African Amanda Coetzer for the mature male.... Serena Williams had biceps like a stevedore's.
- Dressed in a skimpy black number closer in dimensions to a postage stamp than a dress, Kournikova turned heads as she waited on the steps of the Members Stand for the Australians to walk back to their dressing room.... [T]he media fell over themselves to capture the moment or (dare we say it) take a closer look.
- If all the world's a stage, Anna Kournikova wants to be the main act. Make that the *only* act. Never mind that she's only 16 and never been hissed. This walking, talking, Russian-born Barbie look-alike has completed the learning curve.... [She] reduces men aged 15 to 50 to gibbering idiots and ... tells ball boys who want to take her out that they can't afford her.[31]

As we saw in the case of Mauresmo, print and audiovisual media often diverge in their coverage of tennis sexuality. Tennis is the only women's sport that routinely obtains mainstream TV network attention worldwide.[32] But TV tennis talk still awaits its full development. A shot is the tennis equivalent of the sign. Like the latter, the former does not contain meaning—it registers only syntagmatically. Indeed, it is not uncommon for a player to win more points than an opponent, yet lose the set or even the match. The larger tennis phrasings and cadences have yet to make their way into broadcast language. In the meantime, gender provides continuity where a shot-by-shot account cannot. TV announcers, often former professionals, remark on the appearance of women's bodies in a manner that has only the vaguest equivalent in terms of men's "fitness." Seldom is an opportunity lost to remark on how much weight Davenport has shed as an account of her improved performance; Seles's former coach was said to have her weight reduction as his sole function; and Jennifer Capriati's 2001 triumph in Melbourne was attributed to therapy and diet. The body can also be too femme: Hingis is frequently termed a "scrambler" who lacks any "big weapons" but miraculously manages to get the ball back more times than her opponent. On one level, these missives reflect the general impoverishment of tennis announcing, which has neither the descriptive simultaneity of basketball and boxing nor the arch abstractions of statistical buffery in football and baseball. Numbers don't seem to tell as effective a story in tennis as elsewhere, and no narrative form has developed to address what players are doing at any given moment that also accounts for the game's larger temporality.

We might now look at some of these questions via the analysis of a specific text. Consider the Australian network Channel 7's coverage of the 1993 Australian Women's Open. The match between Mary-Jo Fernandez and Shi-Ting Wang on 22 January was described by Gary Wilkinson and Wendy Turnbull, the latter a former champion player. Play was initially even, then Fernandez took control. Camera angles and commentary varied between the exclamatory and the diagnostic, a duality matched by graphic representations of the contest. So a wide-angle long shot, raised above the players from the master position encompassing the length of the court during play, would be interspersed with medium close-ups on the winner of a point from her own level, in between rallies from secondary positions. This set up a dispassionate view from on high versus the emotional reaction supposedly engendered by a concentration on the face. The commentary by Wilkinson was frequently a simple silence during rallies, followed by onomatopeia at the moment of their conclusion to match the stadium reaction, itself captured on actuality audio. The crowd gasped, sighed, and applauded. Wilkinson exclaimed, approved, and instructed: "Voof! Now there's a shot! Gosh!... Well done!... You've gotta hand it to this girl. Gee, she's a fighter.... You've gotta admire this girl." We can see a combination of male hysteria with paternalism in these contributions. Turnbull, by contrast, was technical in her remarks and far more instrumental in her approach: "Good anticipation.... She's certainly mixing it up."

Virtually all of these comments veer between the summative and the predictive. There is no description as such, although where Wilkinson was performative in his statements—they play out his emotions—Turnbull was constative: Her utterances produce a signifying ground of truth and falsehood, offering an opinion that can be agreed with or dissented from. Where Wilkinson has the first call of the director and tends to invite Turnbull to speak, Turnbull has the advantage of additional time to ponder what has occurred and render it intelligible, rather than shrieking out. A similar set of oppositions is in evidence via graphic devices used by the network to represent the state of play and aid diagnosis. A green tennis-ball figure, shaped not unlike the way that commercials for washing powders represented biting enzymes before pollution displaced progress as a trope, became a combination of advanced technology and humorous self-deflation, as per the long shot–close-up/Turnbull–Wilkinson oppositions between scientific objectivity and emotive involvement. The arms of the graphic ball held up signs giving information about the score. Sometimes, the ball itself became a promotional tool, representing the network and its commitment to Australia, with the green figure partially obscured by an Australian flag. The diegesis of the text was displaced by a humorous (but non-ironic) performance of the network's patriotism. Tennis and Channel 7 entered into a synecdochical relationship to Australia, with the simulated ball standing as part of the sport, the network, and the nation. Just as Wilkinson utilized the "right" of men to speak

generically for men and women, and then to act emotively as a
"fan," our representative at the court, Turnbull utilized the right
of experience and expertise to pronounce upon the truth from a
privileged vantage point of both engagement and reason.[33]

As discussed earlier, commentary on women's sports has conventionally focused less on tactics, strategy, and history than on
looks, and has emphasized emotional interiority over skill. Success
and failure are routinely attributed to "feelings," and infantilization
is achieved by referring to women by their first names and men by
their last. U.S. coverage has recently shied away from calling the
competitors "girls," but they remain "Steffis" and "Martinas." Similar trivializing norms are found on Internet discussion groups. The
age discrimination evident in these descriptions is significant—
women turn pro in the month of their fourteenth birthday, and with
numerous cases of anorexia and bulimia reported, there is a real
issue over gender and youthfulness in the sport.[34]

The policing of women's bodies by commentary is complicated
by the very diversity of types that it must describe, especially in
the women's game. Simply looking at who wins, it is much easier to draw the conclusion that corporeal diversity is a resource for
women and not a deficit. If King's off-court appearance was
overdetermined by the *women's* movement, a coterie of present
players have become icons of the *fashion* movement, as noted earlier. Venus Williams has had a line of tennis wear designed for her
that features cutout backs or sides, functionally mimicking haute
couture fashions that highlight the exceptionalism of the women's
bodies that display them. A woman short of the six foot, two inch,
muscularity of Venus Williams would have some difficulty fitting
her togs. Yet Venus's body gets most attention for an incident at
the 1997 U.S. Open semifinal in which she and Irina Spirlea col-
lided during a changeover from one side of the court to the other.
Spirlea is typically seen by reporters as having challenged the
African American teenager to defer to a more experienced player.
Such insouciance extends to talk about Williams's beaded hair,

which rattles, hums, and occasionally falls onto the court. She was docked a point in Melbourne for one such errant bead, which became the opportunity for further comment on her defiant posture. At the same time, Kournikova can be dismissed as unserious because she is a sexual icon. *Sports Illustrated* devoted a cover story to her in 2000, complete with "bedroom"-style shots and a self-reflexive critique for paying so much attention to someone who had never won a tournament on the women's tour.[35] When she ran up a string of double faults at the Australian, but otherwise thoroughly outplayed her opponents to win several matches, she was treated as if she were getting by on looks alone. Hingis, on the other hand, is typically infantilized as a "nice little girl," always smiling and polite, good-natured, precocious but unthreatening, infinitely adaptable to others (and therefore winning by exposing their weaknesses). Her mother, Melanie Molitor, is coach and single parent, and Martina's tennis is taken as evidence of what a fine job Melanie has done raising her daughter. When Hingis behaved like a brat at the French Open in 1999, serving underarm to Graf because she was losing, this was interrogated as a function of deteriorating relations with her mother.

From the Stadium to the Streets

The gendered tennis quotidian is no less replete with issues evident at elite levels. Consider this account of a weekly game by a coauthor of this chapter, Randy Martin:

> A crackling serve sends me wide for a diving backhand return. I just manage to get my racquet on the ball to slice it low over the net. My opponent is there at the net and scoops the ball crosscourt. I tear after it and send it sailing high for a defensive lob. No avail. An overhead smash puts the ball definitively out of reach. If I were to break the protocols of play, take my eye off the ball, and regard the person I'm playing with, I'd know right away she's a woman. But within the point, it's certainly not clear what makes for the gender divide between us. Is it the net? A binary

machinery if ever there was one, literally painting partners into separate boxes. The arsenal of shots and the longer *durée* of strategy convert differences taken as axiomatic off the court into calibrations of points won and lost for reasons of their own. The person I'm playing, Michele Machee, has an all-court game: deeply penetrating topspin groundstrokes, unerring serves that clip the back of the line, savvy net-rushing that yields crisp angled volleys, fine court coverage, and the patience and perseverance to make the point on the third or fourth shot. She was a top player on her Texas State Championship-winning high school team. While growing up she never found it complimentary to be told, "Wow, you don't play like a girl." Michele observed that in the days of John McEnroe and Evert, net-play divided the men's and women's games, but not today. That poses the question, aside from the tautology that women's tennis is tennis played by women, where does the gender of the game lie?

The contradictions of commodified, gendered tennis do not fit an ideal–typical functionalist landscape of docile, hyperfeminine women fresh (albeit perhaps glowing) from country-club lawns. *That* tennis was caught in a vise of the sort discarded when warpable wood racquets were replaced with synthetic fibers and carbon. The ad campaign for the 1998 U.S. Open made direct comparisons with football and basketball, asserting that tennis players ran farther and longer, in effect playing harder. In this newly universalized sporting aesthetic, tennis toughness was a virtue. Men and women were featured in commercials grunting, hurtling, and smashing. Six months later, Mauresmo gambled— and the power in the game is likely to be something she gets a slice of. The personalization of tennis stars, the storytelling that is part of WTA marketing and broadcasting, had a visual spot for her significant other in the stands.

Four weeks after meeting in Melbourne, Hingis and Mauresmo played again, in the quarterfinals of the Gaz de France Open, where the local media referred to Bourdon as Mauresmo's *"petite amie"* (little friend). This time, the result was reversed, with Mauresmo winning. The crowd held banners reading, "We love you

Amélie" and "We're behind you Amélie" and hissed and booed her opponent during introductions and the warm-up. Their next rematch, at the French Open in May 1999, was another victory for Hingis, with strenuous crowd opposition and the victor asserting that Mauresmo's muscular development prevented her from having a "feel on court." But Mauresmo has the prospect of coming out a winner. She proudly told Gerd Czoppelt, who maintains her fan Web site, "*Sylvie c'est 50% de mes victoires*" ("Sylvie brings me half my success")—this on a Web site formerly replete with images of the two women topless together, alongside affectionate, fully clothed pictures. Meanwhile, U.S. Open advertising could not decide what impeded her progress up the rankings: "errant volleys" or "questions from the media about her lesbian lifestyle." Not surprisingly, Mauresmo has become a heroine in the lesbian media, receiving front-page coverage and accolades in *Curve* magazine.[36] And despite some virulent homophobic attacks in the mainstream press, she appeared on *Stade 2*, a popular sports show on French TV, after her match at Gaz de France Open; a few hours later she was the featured guest on French TV's most prestigious prime-time commercial news program; shortly thereafter, Mauresmo and Bourdon appeared on the front cover of the highly popular glossy magazine *Paris-Match*, followed by eight pages of photos and interviews; and when the French prime minister invited 100 women to a formal function to celebrate International Women's Day 2000, Bourdon accompanied Mauresmo.

Conclusion

Booters with Hooters

The implications here are not that the players [on the 1999 U.S. Women's World Cup soccer team] are sexually available, but that they are "normal," that they are proper role models for all the girls who will buy shoes and gear (and eventually cosmetics that won't run or cake late in the match?). For the World Cup team to crack into the male-dominated merchandising mart as a group and as individuals, they must dispel the aura of homosexuality that was hung on women's athleticism as a way of stifling their emerging physical and political power . . . a betrayal of all the lesbians. —*Robert Lipsyte (1999a)*

n 1996, no room could be found in NBC's stable to cover women's soccer at the Atlanta Olympic Games. But three years later, the winning U.S. women's World Cup soccer squad dubbed themselves "booters with hooters" and delivered the best local ratings ever for soccer, men's or women's, and for any women's sporting event, not to mention filling Giants Stadium with more people than the NFL ever had. They even outdrew the TV audience for the NBA finals. Total crowd attendance outstripped that for any women's sports event anywhere. Within minutes of receiving their medals, the team had shot two commercials for Disney. The *New York Times* reacted to intense criticism of a columnist's claim that sports were all about sex after the Cup by belatedly allowing drugs and violence their place on the spectrum. Meanwhile, a U.S. federal lawsuit was in play over accusations by the former college soccer player Kathleen Peay that her coach at Oklahoma had hazed freshmen by forcing them to "wear diapers and simulate fellatio on bananas" and be "photographed with pickles in their mouths." The coach, Bettina Fletcher, did not comment.[1]

There can be no better encapsulation of the ambivalence of Sportsex. On the one hand lies the grotesque sexism of reducing women to breast size associated with the word "hooters." On the other is a sense of sexual, sporting, and cultural power that comes from this improbable rhyming syntagm. At the moment of crisis, when the final penalty shot in the final was successful, Brandi "Hollywood" Chastain tore her shirt off, revealing a Nike sports bra as she fell to the ground in ecstasy—providing a cover shot for *Time* and *Newsweek* in the process (19 July 1999), along with numerous promotional opportunities set up by her sponsor Nike to disclaim any intended product placement. As she put it: "In front of 90,185 people in the stadium and 40 million TV viewers, I ripped off my shirt. As I lifted it off, I lifted all the expectations and pressure off winning." The following week, Nike held a press conference in midtown Manhattan. Chastain was asked how she felt about being a sex symbol. She replied that she was uncertain of the meaning of the term. She might be one "if it means feeling good about yourself," and she rejoiced at no longer shying away from wearing bikinis around the pool.

This naïveté was touchingly improbable, given Chastain's posing nude in *Gear* magazine's sex issue prior to the World Cup, following which she had responded to critics by saying, "Hey, I ran my ass off for this body."[2] Chastain's act caught the attention of David Letterman, host of the internationally syndicated *Late Show* on CBS. He invited her on the program and subsequently became an unofficial cheerleader for the squad each night by showing a signed photograph of the team in which the players wore *Late*

Show T-shirts and nothing else. He proclaimed them "Soccer Mamas" and "Babe City."

By exposing her Inner Active Sports Bra, Chastain gave Nike, which supplied the American team with its sportswear, an incalculable sales boost in the United States' $500 million a year sports-bra market; she also enhanced Nike's already widespread brand-name recognition. Although Chastain's behavior was spontaneous, Nike's presence was not. At the time, the company had personal contracts with six members of the American team and ran several TV ads featuring its players during the month-long World Cup. Nike was also reported to be negotiating for the rights to use photos of Chastain that appeared on the front pages of virtually every American newspaper.

The predominantly white composition of the team also came under scrutiny, with the executive editor of HarperCollins, which published a book by one of the team's star players, Mia Hamm, commenting that: "The question needs to be asked, would this team be receiving all this attention if they looked like the Brazilian women's national team—boyish, wholly unglamorous and black?" The always already sexualized female sporting body becomes more or less valorized according to its relationship to prescribed modes of Anglo hyperfemininity. *Sports Illustrated for Women* featured several top players alongside Chastain mimicking her famous pose, blending pumped muscles and sports bras. *Sports Illustrated* for everybody named the players sports identities of the year—the second time the honor had gone to a team.[3] The front-cover team picture had an unusual parallel inside the magazine, which featured historic photos of the players as children—infantalization at the moment of triumph. And 2000 was marked by the Australian women's soccer team's releasing a nude calendar. In 1999, the U.S. women's track-and-field team provided many models for a nude photographic session, along with Paralympians. The year of the Sydney Olympics saw many members of the U.S. team involved in nude shots apart from the soccer players—notably, the swimmers Jenny Thompson, Amy Van Dyken, Angel Marino, and Dara Torres. Such male sports stars as Dan O'Brien and Ricky Williams also posed naked.[4]

Across town, a letter-writer to the *Toronto Star* suggested that "if Mauresmo's one-handed backhand is comparable to Pete Sampras' then who is to say that Sampras isn't playing like a girl?" Of course, Sampras has also been aced by Alexandra Stevenson in practice. Then the closing stages of the century featured the first modern professional cross-gender boxing bout to be officially licensed, ending in a unanimous points decision in favor of the woman. And women's bouts are now obligatory components of any U.S. pay-per-view card.[5] Meanwhile, an investment-services firm was advertising itself via a commercial featuring Mary-Jo Fernandez and Anna Kournikova. Fernandez opens the text by stating that she's not close to Kournikova. We cut to the latter, who is explaining high finance on court to a group of children, then move to a glamorous take of her in a red dress with her hair down. Fernandez comments that players are jealous "of her [Kournikova's] portfolio."

In other words, this cosmic gender ambivalence has become part of capital's own, ironized delivery. Consider a 1999 U.S. television commercial for Adidas. It shows a white businessman in the back of a New York cab, whingeing and whining about Yankees baseball and how much he loathes the Bronx Bombers. The driver is not identified, but he is Sunil Gavaskar—unintelligible to the majority of the TV audience, but readable by South Asian taxi drivers and audiences as the most storied batsman in Indian cricket history. He deposits the business leach in a derelict neighborhood for an assignation with someone coded as a transsexual prostitute. As Gavaskar drives off laughing, the final shot of the sequence discloses that his cab bears a Yankee license plate, and we are drawn to the premium cable network HBO's series of true-life candid photos of taxis and their late-night denizens. The Fox Sports Network promotes its 2000 game show with a shot of a teenage boy gawking at a woman breastfeeding in his train compartment. She asks him, "Excuse me. Who's the only MVP to play for a losing Super Bowl team?" In their latent and manifest levels of address and content, these commercials bear witness to the complex intermeshing of global, local, and sexual, as sports make their contradictory way somewhere among civil society, marketplace, and unrepresentative demagoguery—always collective, however commodified they may become.

Time hailed the "booters with hooters" as a sign that "heroin chic" in advertising was over, trumped by the team's captain, Julie Foudy, posing (with husband) for *Sports Illustrated*'s "swimsuit issue," Chastain in *Gear*, and Hamm agreeing to be one of *People* magazine's fifty "most beautiful people"—not to mention Kournikova all over. Of course, the soccer player and fundamentalist Christian Michelle Akers pronounced herself "a bit uncomfortable" with this sexiness, but we could all be mollified by the double-branding of Foudy, Chastain, and Hamm by Letterman as "Soccer Mamas," thanks to their heteronormative familial arrangements. This was in keeping with the insistent focus of *Sports Illustrated for Women* (Summer 1999) on the honeymoons, weddings, and children of the players, and the *Wall Street Journal*'s certainty that their soccer success was due to skill, not Title IX. This line of reasoning was aided by the Gatorade commercial that pitted Hamm against Michael Jordan, one-on-one, to the tune of Irving Berlin's "Anything You Can Do, I Can Do Better," from the musical *Annie Get Your Gun*. C. L. Cole mockingly calls this "democracy in action; the only limits . . . those imposed on the self by the self." That fall, 44 percent of U.S. teenagers voted Hamm "hottest athlete" in a React.com poll, with second-place-winner Kobe Bryant attracting 16 percent of the vote.[6] Who needs affirmative action with selves like these on the loose?

On the other hand, the fate of the women's team after the World Cup gave pause to those who would attribute its success to individualism rather than collaborative politics. The team organized its own indoor tour following the Cup because the pay was higher than offered for an official trip, and it refused to tour Australia later that year over a wage dispute ($3,150 a month for the tour). After controversy over the reappointment of the team's coach, Tony DiCicco, he declined to stand. For the first time, the U.S. Soccer Federation appointed a woman, April Heinrichs, as head coach. But she was widely seen as an antidote to the players' attempts to secure improved pay and conditions: "See what happens when women play sports? They want to make a living wage." As for the team's iconic status, media attention to women's soccer remains insignificant outside the United States, China, and Scandinavia.[7] A rematch between the United States and the People's Republic of China in 2000 drew 550 spectators in Australia.

Many critics condemn the display of sportswomen in sexualized poses, viewing this not as an expression of power and self-confidence on their part, but as a backlash by the media to trivialize women and hence marginalize their gains in the social sphere.[8] These limits reference certain caveats that must be placed on my embrace of sexual commodification, given the dominant allegorization of sports. That semiotic system routinely cross-validates the market and the nation via myths of representativeness, justice, and upward mobility. These myths idealize existing politics, economics, and the social, distorting conflict, then resignifying it. Richard Hoggart identifies such qualities as crucial to the appeal professional sports hold for working people: the capacity to make politics both personal and concrete.[9]

The complex double-declutching between the personal immediacy of sports and their collective symbolic power has to be evaluated for the costs to those who comply with or refuse them. The left can draw on sports as an ethical, intertextual center—as dominant discourse has done. To assist the process, we need to do work that analyzes business, the body, television, and the nation, encompassing the principal discursive formations of the phenomenon. I think of these as concerned with sports *qua* entertainment, education, political symbol, and science in experienced, governed, and commercial forms. This requires a combination of political economy, textual analysis, and ethnography across the sports media, amateur and professional organizations, international agencies, and corporations, tracking the commodification and governmentalization of bodies. Such work could make for some reciprocity between sports and mainstream sociocultural theory. Developments in global capitalism toward the effacement of divisions between production and circulation enter the agenda, too. Sports show how the body is an always already mediated object, rearticulated with the supposed essence of the person via training and play. Sports stars instantiate the possibilities and limitations of life within formal and informal rules and expectations. The sports watcher's body, too, in its visceral reaction to events of great moment on-screen or at a stadium, is a crucial site of public commitment and energy, frequently in destructive and violent ways. This key cultural technology can have its meanings changed if these iterative moves turn away from competition and hierarchy and toward collaboration and exchange (equally valued aspects of most sports).

Sporting spectatorship and participation have significant, positive aspects. Yes, narcissism, a high component of commodification, intense sexist pressure about body image, and unpleasant associations with militarism and Tayloristic discipline are dominant. But there is also a physical pleasure and ecstasy that can come with the melding of individual and collaborative striving and watching in sports, a phenomenal form that merges the empirical–transcendental couplet. This has meant a certain reclamation of public and private health from a male-dominated medical establishment; criticism of fast-food and cigarette capitalism; and the generation of new, non-competitive sports alternatives that connect to environmental awareness and experience. Much dominant allegorization of sports embodies and enables the exercise of gendered power. At the same time, the very process of commodification, in all its tentacular drive, has truly transformative effects on the play of sex and gender in sports. That new complexity has animated the studies in this book.

The message of *Sportsex* is that good cultural politicians must know the importance of sporting terrain. Take Saint Paul (*Corinthians* 1, chap. 9), who gave sports a key role in self-denial:

> Know ye not that they which run in a race run all, but one receiveth the prize? So run, that ye may obtain. And every man that striveth for the mastery is temperate in all things. Now they do it to obtain a corruptible crown; but we are incorruptible. I therefore so run, not as uncertainly; so fight I, not as one that beateth the air: But I keep under my body, and bring it into subjection: lest that by any means, when I have preached to others, I myself should be a castaway.

The first Olympic Games were professional: In fifth-century B.C. Athens, victory in a sprint brought a man enough money to live comfortably for three years.[10] For Paul, a business matter—winning the prize—was also a sign of self-mastery, especially for those wont to breach what they preach. This combination of finance with ethics is crucial: The body becomes simultaneously a source of success, a site of reward, and a subject of rule. In the sector of latter-day multinational capitalism dedicated to First World culture industries, these forces are at play in myriad contradictory forms, as the gazing spectator's money turns self-control into public display and transforms gender politics along the way. Saint Paul is back on the road to Damascus, and he doesn't like what he sees.

Notes

Introduction

1. Advertisement, *New York Times* (3 June 1999), A19.
2. Morse 1983, 44.
3. McKay and Huber 1992, 208.
4. Klein 1995, 105.
5. Drape 1999.
6. Morse 1983, 44.
7. Smith 1996.
8. McCarthy 1995; Wenner 1998, 326; Eastman and Land 1997.
9. Houlihan 1994, 164; Cooper 1995, 72–4; Brodeur 1988, 233; Lurie 1994, 123–4; Savan 1994, 225; Hall 1993, 56.
10. Duquin 1998.
11. Halberstam 1998.
12. Hall 1997, 233.
13. Thompson 1999.
14. Poynton and Hartley 1990, 144.
15. Carroll 1999.
16. Seabrook 1997.
17. Century 2000.
18. Burstyn 1999, 137.
19. Mazer 1998, 118.
20. Early 1996, 7.
21. Lipsyte 1999a, 1999b.

Chapter 1

1. Hargreaves 1986, 13. See also Messner 1988; Trujillo 1991; D. Andrews 1993; Cole 1993; Gruneau 1993; Heikkala 1993.
2. Bartky 1988; Bordo 1990.

3. Kroker et al., 1989.
4. Layden 1999a; McDowell 1999–2000a.
5. Featherstone et al. 1991; Kirk 1993; Shilling 1993.
6. Shilling 1991, 665.
7. Grosz 1987, 9; Gatens 1988.
8. Foucault 1986, 66–9.
9. Ibid., 72.
10. Ibid., 72–7, 104, 120, 197–8, 212.
11. Foucault 1988, 56–7.
12. Ibid., 238–9.
13. Stratton 1986; Horrocks 1995, 149; Hearn 1992, 215.
14. "A Brief History of Sex" 2000, 31.
15. Alter 1995; Klein 1995; Marshall and Cook 1992, 308; Moss et al. 1993; Sabo 1993, 7; Lueschen 1993, 97; "Stopping" 1999; Bamberger and Yaeger 1997; Pope et al. 2000, xiii.
16. Elias 1986b, 19–21, 38–9; idem 1986a, 165, 173–4, 150–1, 155, 159.
17. Eichberg 1986.
18. Hall 1993, 51; Loy et al. 1993, 70.
19. Lasch 1979, 181–2, 185.
20. Butler 1998, 109–11.
21. Fiddes 1991, 176–7; Park 1994, 70; Hargreaves 1986, 30–1, 48; Dewar 1993, 151–7; Hall 1993; Mitchell and Dyer 1985, 96–7.
22. Cole 1993, 87–90.
23. Rowe 1997b, 123; idem, "Out of Bounds" 1996, 1050.
24. Messner 1990, 213.
25. "Catching Up" 1999–2000; Billings, 1999–2000.
26. Hall 1981.
27. Disch and Kane 1996; McKay 1992; Ndalianis 1995; White and Gillett 1994.
28. Guttmann 1994, 132; de Moragas Spà et al. 1995, 22; Kinnick 1998, 212–3.
29. Longman 2000, 1, 24.
30. Jarvie and Maguire 1994, 161; Sage 1998, 68, 72; M. A. Hall 1999, 3; S. Smith 1999; Williams 2000; E. Anderson 1999, 85.
31. Wright 1991; Ryan 1996.
32. Fussell 1993, 577; Morse 1983, 45; weightlifter quoted in Shilling 1994, 144; Klein 1995.
33. Flannery 1996; Foss 1985, 8.
34. Lewis 1985, 23.
35. Berkman 1999; Woog 1998; Martin 1999; Lipsyte 1999c, 1999e; Pettitte as quoted in Olney 1999.
36. Smith 2000.

37. Nack and Yaeger 1999, 45

38. Reed 1994, 24; Pener 1994, 28; Blinde and Taub 1992; Solomon et al. 1999.

39. "Brady's" 1999.

40. Cahn 1994, 246, 266; Jefferson Lenskyj 1998; Marchese 1993; Feder 1994.

41. Benton 1991; Featherstone et al. 1991; Falk 1994; Loy et al. 1993, 75.

42. Allison 1994, 92; Arbena 1993, 110–2; Shapiro 1989, 71, 74; Kennedy, as quoted in Lasch 1979, 183.

43. Recreation and sport minister, as quoted in Volkerling 1994, 8; Agnew and Petersen 1989; McMurtry 1993, 422; Griffin 1993, 119; Scraton 1987, 169–71, 174.

44. Tudor 1992; O'Donnell 1998; Skillen 1993, 350; U.S. Peace Corps representative, as quoted in Kang 1988, 1, 43.

45. Shapiro 1989, 80, 87; McKay 1992, 256; Ronald Reagan, as quoted in Monnington 1993.

46. Rowe and Lawrence 1986, 196–7.

47. Gledhill 1991, xiii–xiv; Cawelti 1980, 10; Watson 1973, 16, 19, n. 19.

48. King 1987, 151–2.

49. Bale 1991, 74, 79; Cahn 1994, 269–71; Rowe and Brown 1994, 101; Jiobu 1988; Lapchick and Benedict 1993.

50. Lumpkin and Williams 1991; Chisholm 1999, 135.

51. Tebbitt quoted in Marquesee 1994, 137–8.

52. Jarvie and Maguire 1994, 175; Guttmann 1994, 129; Vines 1988, 49.

53. Hornung 1936, 13.

54. Smith 1996, 2.

55. As quoted in Schreier 1989, 104.

56. As quoted in Mass–Observation 1939, 133.

57. McKay 1997, 118.

58. Duncan and Messner 2000.

59. Messner et al. 1993; McKay and Huber 1992; Schulze 1990; Bale 1991, 90; Nelson 1994; Dewar 1993, 155; Cahn 1994, 260–1, 254–7; Bamberger and Yaeger 1997; *Time* magazine, as quoted in Ellsworth 1986, 47.

60. Duncan 1990; Eitzen 1999, 24.

61. Burstyn 1999, 103; Cagan 1999.

62. Leath and Lumpkin 1992; McKay 1995; Sabo and Jansen 1992, 170.

63. Whannel 1999, 257.

64. L. R. Davis 1997.

65. Reichert et al. 1999; Dyer 1992, 104; Embrey et al. 1992, 12.

66. Messner et al. 1993; M. A. Hall 1999.

67. Miller 1990, 78–82.
68. Poynton and Hartley 1990, 150.
69. As quoted in Sparks 1992, 330, 334; "There's Life Outside Sports" 1998.
70. Sargenti et al. 1998, 47; Daddario 1997, 104; Ryan 1996, 2–3; "Sport" 1995; Remnick 1996, 27; Kinnick 1998, 212–3; Chisholm 1999, 126; "Demo Derby" 1998; M. A. Hall 1999, 4; Elliott 1998b, C9; Tuggle and Owen 1999; Eastman and Billings 1999; Walker 1999; Adalian 1998; Boal 1999, 42; King 1999; Nelson 1999.
71. Wenner and Gantz 1998, 235; Daddario 1997, 103–4.
72. Morse 1983, 44–6.
73. As quoted in Tudor 1992, 397.
74. As quoted in ibid., 400–1.
75. Morris and Nydahl 1985, 105; Bryant et al. 1977.
76. Hitchcock 1991, 75.
77. Quoted in Benaud 1984, 117.
78. Heuring 1988, 90; *Open the Box* 1986; Edgerton and Ostroff 1985, 276.
79. As quoted in Miller 1989, 594.
80. Hitchcock 1991, 76.
81. Geurens 1989, 57–8, 61; Mazer 1998, 114.

Chapter 2

1. Kimmel 1992; Connell 1992, 735.
2. Gramsci 1978, 12.
3. Connell 1987, 1993, 1995 (pp. 185–99), 1996, 1998.
4. Cahn 1993, 344.
5. McKay 1991, 55.
6. Schwartz 1997, 56.
7. As quoted in T. W. Smith 1999.
8. As quoted in Eitzen 1990, 84.
9. Messner 1997, 7–8, 12; Rowe 1997b, 124.
10. Connell 1990, 1995.
11. K. Davis 1997, 555, 563; Badinter 1995, 25–6; Kimmel 1992, 167.
12. Coleman 1990, 193, 196; see also Wetherell and Edley 1999.
13. Seabrook 1997, 44.
14. Sacks 1995, 568.
15. See McHoul 1997 for an application of this thesis to sports.
16. Hannah Arendt, as quoted in Gross 1991, 377; D. A. Miller 1992, 41; Hall 1991, 54; Adams and Cowie 1990.
17. Pronger 1990, 178.

18. Badinter 1995, 32–3.
19. Barratt and Straus 1994, 43–5.
20. Girard 1992, 145–9.
21. Kimmel 1992, 162.
22. Rowe 1997b, 124–5.
23. Pronger 1990, 181.
24. Rowe 1997b, 127; Horrocks 1995, 152; Carlton 1997.
25. Pronger 1990, 190; Poynton and Hartley 1990, 151, 156.
26. Fox 1989; Nixon 1996, 96–9.
27. Hamilton 2000, F1, F4.
28. Rawlings 1993; Alsop 1999a, 1999b; Cahill 1997, 34; O'Connor 1997; Bank 1999, B1; Elliott 1998a; Rutenberg and Elliott 2000.
29. Deacon 1998.
30. Burstyn 1999, 218–9; Gluckman and Reed 1997; Alsop 1999c.
31. Baker 2000, 17–19.
32. Dyer 1992, 104; Harari 1993; Barham 1985, 62; Burke 1999; Jenkins 1998, 92; Hamermesh and Biddle 1994; Wells 1991; Freudenheim 1999; Lemon 1997a, 30; Bordo 1998, 217; S. S. Hall 1999, 33; "Marketplace" 1999; Burstyn 1999, 217; Stein 1999; Wheeler 1999; Pope et al. 2000, xiii, 12, 18, 27, 31, 43, 47, 54; Tien 1999.
33. Shoebridge 1989, 164; *Sydney Morning Herald*, as quoted in Huxley 1989; Sleeman 1990, 11; Davidson as quoted in Roveré 1990.
34. Officials as quoted in Shoebridge 1989; Quayle as quoted in Oram at Large 1990, 8, and in Lynch and May 1989, 50; Pearce and Campbell 1993, 18; Advertisement, *Variety* (15–21 September 1997), 27; Cox and Fullagar 1992, 22.
35. McKay 1997, 97.
36. Carmichael 1992, 107, 109, 120–1; Cashman 1995, 73, 76–7, 87.
37. Cashman 1995, 87; officials as quoted in Stoddart 1986, 143.
38. Pronger 1990, 31–2, 270; Stewart as quoted in Daddario 1997, 107.
39. BBC as quoted in Peters 1976, 127; Higgs and Weiller 1994, 242–3.
40. Webster quoted in Wright 1991, 61–2; Kingston 1990, 83.
41. Budd 1989; Bale 1991.
42. "Laurie Lawrence Profile" n.d.
43. Tomlinson and Yorganci 1997, 134; Ryan 1996; Armstrong as quoted in *Daily Telegraph* 1996; Murphy, n.d.
44. Available from www.bigpond.com/community/chat/events/duncanarmstrong.asp.
45. Denizet-Lewis 1999.
46. Villarosa 1994, 18; Clark 1994; Schaap 1994, 33; Curran 1998; Krane and Romont 1997.

47. Rowe 1997b, 127; Curry 1991; Connell 1992, 741; Spitzack 1998, 151–2; P. Griffin 1998, 22; Mariscal 1999.

48. Lipsyte 1997; "Breaking the Silence" 1999.

49. Stockwell and McAuley 1996, 54; Name withheld by request 1997; Solomon et al. 1999; Frey 1994; Rowe 1997b, 127; Pener 1994; "White Appears" 1998; Youngblood 1998.

50. Fornoff 1993, 175; jeering crowds as quoted in van Tiggelen 1999, 25–6; Hanlon 1998; Knitting Circle n.d.; "A Time" 1998; John Fashanu, as quoted in Hanlon 1998; "Are You a Victim" 1998; Bletchley 1998a, 1998b; "Sauna" 1998; Watson-Smyth 1998; Newkey-Burden 1998.

51. "Anger" 1999; Randall 1999; Williams 1999; "SOCC" 1999; Banks quoted in "Gay Plagued League Star" 1998.

52. Lipsyte 1991; U.S. state senator as quoted in Berkow 1997; Simmons 1997, 46; Hall as quoted in Cahn 1993, 343; Pichler and Louganis 1997; "Breaking the Silence" 1999; Lemon 1997b; Pela 1997; E. Anderson 1999, 28; Coakley 1999, 286.

53. Kirby 1986; Pronger 1990, xi; Lemon 1997a; Flaherty 1999; Rowe 1997b, 129.

54. Solomon 1994, 4; Champagne 1996, 50–1; Messner 1997, 81–3; Mercer and Julien 1992, 42.

55. Dunne 1997, 10.

56. Cashman 1995, 81.

57. T. Miller 1998, 108–13, 132–7.

58. Hunt 2000; Ryan as quoted in Freeman 1997, 45; *Mirror* as quoted in Dunne 1997, 10; Wilkins 1996, 198, 200.

59. Roberts 1997; Freeman 1997, 1–9, 26.

60. Freeman 1997, 31, 54, 72–4; Connell 1996, 170–1.

61. Piggins as quoted in Freeman 1997, 82; Armstrong 1998, 157; Freeman 1997, 168–70, 187, 240,.

62. Palmer 1997; Freeman 1997, 274–6, 307–10, 321; Dunne 1997, 12; "Gay Plagued League Star" 1998; Roberts quoted in Burfitt 1996; Page 1997; Denizet-Lewis 1999; Thévenin 1997.

63. Available from www.gaygate.com/media/speak2/ian.shtml.

64. "Gays and the Australian Economy" 1999.

65. Roberts as quoted in West 1997, Dunne 1997 (p. 13), and Burfitt 1996; "Help" 1999; Weidler 1999.

66. Rogers 2000, 59.

67. Chambers 1999; GLINN n.d.

Chapter 3

1. Lapchick with Matthews, n.d., 25–6.

2. Boyd 1997; McKay 1995; D. Andrews 1996a, 1996b; Andrews et al. 1996; Rowe 1994.

3. Lynd and Lynd 1956, 212–3, 485; Jarvie and Maguire 1994, 19; Agnew and Petersen 1989; McMurtry 1993, 422; Messner 1997, 28–9.

4. Lynd and Lynd 1965, 291–2; Cobb 1993; "Out of Bounds" 1996.

5. Andrews 1996–97, 57.

6. Pereira 1996.

7. Morrison 1997, xiv.

8. Begel and Baum 2000, 50–1; Benedict 1998, xi–xii, 1–2; Wahl and Wertheim 1998, 67–8, 71; "Irresponsible Athletes" 1998.

9. Rodman with Keown 1996, 245; Galvin 1997; Berkow 1998; Mercer and Julien 1992, 43.

10. Rodman with Keown 1996, 179, 198, 216; Cherfils 1999; Lafrance and Rail 2000.

11. Jackson 1998a, 1998b; Jackson et al. 1998; Simson and Jennings 1992; Wieland 1993; "Stars" 1998; Kroker et al. 1989, 172.

12. "Group" 1999; "Johnson Wants to Run" 1996; "Johnson's Appeal Denied" 1999; "Johnson Fails" 1999; Buffery 1999a, 1999b.

13. Farber 1996; Jackson "1998a, 26, 28; Colombo 1994; Johnson as quoted in Crary 1998.

14. Athreya 1998; "Pound" 1999; "Ben Johnson" 1998; "Johnson Demeans" 1998; "Two Horses" 1998.

15. McKay 1991; Nittve 1987.

16. Simson and Jennings 1992, 169, 195; Gross 1999; Hall 1997, 228.

17. King 1993; Rowe 1994.

18. O'Neill 1990.

19. Williamson 1988, 5.

20. Treichler 1987, 1999 (pp. 73, 85); Dworkin and Wachs 1998, 6.

21. Harper 1996, 3.

22. Crimp 1993; McKay 1993.

23. Johnson and Johnson 1991, 22.

24. "Hockey Teams" 1991, 7.

25. Swift 1991, 40–3; Elson 1991, 59–60; "Scoring" 1999.

26. Treichler 1988, 220; Johnson as quoted in Ryan 1992, 46, 55; Ryan 1992, 49.

27. Crimp 1993; Harper 1996, 24–5, 32; Dworkin and Wachs 1998, 3, 20, n. 16.

28. "Magic Makes" 1996; Hole 1992, 1–2; Araton 1992, 30; Magic Johnson Foundation n.d.

29. Messner and Solomon 1993. For a more groupie-centered view, see Gmelch and San Antonio 1998

30. Durie 1992.

31. Bordo 1998, 238; R. Miller 1992, 3.

32. Taslitz 1996; Kimmel 1995.

33. "Tyson Released" 1999; "Protestors" 2000.

34. Tyson as quoted in Sloop 1997, 112; see also Jefferson 1997, 1998; Lule 1995; Sloop 1997, 112.

35. Barak 1996; Chancer 1998.

36. Dyson 1993; Wallace 1991.

37. Wallace 1991.

38. Wells 1991, 70.

39. McKay and Smith 1995; Rowe 1997a.

40. Girard 1992, 145–9.

41. Messner 1997, 65; Sailes 1996–97, 6.

42. Farred 1996; Messner 1997, 107; Ross 1998, 25, 97, 111, 168.

Chapter 4

1. Leand 1999.

2. "Amélie Mauresmo fait son come-out." Available from: www.media-g.net/dossiers/cultureg/mauresmo/mauresmo.stm.

3. Mauresmo quoted in *Washington Times* 1999.

4. Hingis as quoted in Layden 1999b; Dillman 1999c; Araton 1999; "No. 1" 1999; Dillman 1999b.

5. *Herald Sun* as quoted in Layden 1999b.

6. Clarey 1999; Dillman 1999a; Naughton 1999.

7. Mauresmo quoted in "Out in the Open" 1999 and Clarey 1999; Navratilova with Vecsey 1985, 55; Roberts 1999; "Gorgeous Women" 1999.

8. Weir 1999; J. Young television as quoted in Dutter and Parsons 1999; "TEN: French" 1999.

9. Birrell and Cole 1994, 373; Blue 1995, 11.

10. Spencer 1997, 373, 375; Evert quoted in Leader 1999; Wenner 1993, 76.

11. Chase 1988; Young 1997; McKay 1997; Ndalianis 1995; White and Gillett 1994; Berlage 1992, 150.

12. Steiner 2000.

13. Bolin 1992, 381–2; M. A. Hall 1999, 11; see also Cole 1993, 88, and Pronger 1998; Layden 1999b.

14. King quoted in Spencer 1997, 375; Davis 1997; Mikosza and Phillips 1999; Deutsher 1999; Jefferson Lenskyj 1998, 31.

15. Hargreaves 1994, 54; Vannier and Poindexter 1960, 253; Lichtenstein 1998, 59.

16. Griffin 1998, 32; Lenskyj 1986, 26, 29–30, 36–7, 39, 44.

17. Cahn 1994, 31, 49–50; Lichtenstein 1998, 61, 63; Hall 1996, 101.

18. Goss 1943, 309, 310, 343.

19. Miller and Ley 1956, 239–70; Vannier and Poindexter 1960, 257; Cahn 1994, 176–9, 182–3, 196.

20. Lichtenstein 1998, 64; King as quoted in Schinto 1994, 24.

21. Lichtenstein 1998, 57, 65.

22. Creedon 1998, 96; Young 1997; Schinto 1994, 25; Young 1999; Brown 1993, 13.

23. Lurie 1994, 120, 123–4, 126; Thompson 1999, 249; Kort 1994, 134; Sandoz 1995; Navratilova with Vecsey 1985, 5; Blue 1995, 90, 101.

24. "Amélie quería ser un hombre" 1999.

25. Burroughs et al. 1995; Lenskyj 1991; Brownworth 1994, 75–6; Lurie 1994, 121; Mandlikova quoted in Cahn 1994, 2; "TEN: Stevenson" 1999; Price 1999, 88; Griffin 1998, 58; Navratilova and Nickles 1996; Paretsky 1995: 130, 143, 147; Bledsoe 1997, 183.

26. Sloan 1994, 95; Lenskyj 1991, 63; Lopiano 1998, viii; Kane and Jefferson Lenskyj 1998, 190; Griffin 1998, 7–8; Galst 1998; Markula 1999.

27. Galst 1998; Rogers 1994, xiv, xvi. See also Lenskyj 1991; Fusco 1998; Hall 1995, 231–3. Guthrie and Castelnuovo 1999; Fish 1998; Connor as quoted in P. Griffin 1998, 62.

28. Zimet 1994, 113; Zwerman 1995; Macdonald 1997, 184; Pitts 1997.

29. Spencer 1997, 364–8, 370, 376.

30. Kane and Jefferson Lenskyj 1998, 189; Kournikova as quoted in "Power Players" 1999; "*Si*view" 1999.

31. Hogan 1998; MacDonald 1998; Gatt 1998; Evans 1998.

32. Daddario 1997, 103; Tuggle 1997, 20–1.

33. Clarke and Clarke 1982, 74.

34. Bruce 1998, 377; Duncan and Messner 1998, 177, 181, 183; Schinto 1994, 24.

35. Deford 2000.

36. Media as quoted in Atkin 1999; Leand and Smith 1999; Hingis as quoted in "Hingis Prevails" 1999; *US Open Tennis Magazine* 1999, 36.

Conclusion

1. Vecsey 1999; Bailey 1999; "Go Figure" 1999; Heywood 2000, ix; McDowell 1999–2000b; "Days" 1999; Lipsyte 1999b; "Oklahoma Crude" 1999.

2. Mead 1999; Chastain as quoted in Lusetich 1999, 53; Voepel 1999.

3. Hamm quoted in Longman "Pride" C23, 1999; also see Penner 1999; Colson 1999. Rasmusson 1999–2000.

4. "Naked Truth" 2000; Reilly 2000.

5. Patel 1999; Price 1999, 89; Verhovek 1999; "Woman Beats Man" 1999; M. A. Hall 1999; Halbert 1997.

6. Sullivan 1999; Longman 1999a, D1; "The Girls" 1999; Cole 2000, 4; "Go Figure" 1999–2000.

7. Sandomir 1999; Longman 1999b, 2000; Pucin 1999; O'Neill 1999.

8. Cagan 2000, 182.

9. Hoggart 1971.

10. Skillen 1993, 349.

Works Cited

"A Brief History of Sex." 2000. *Sports Illustrated* (8 May), 31.

Adalian, Josef. 1998. "ABC in Pigskin Pickle." *Daily Variety Gotham* (30 December), 1, 17.

Adams, Parveen, and Elizabeth Cowie, eds. 1990. *The Woman in Question*. Cambridge, Mass.: MIT Press.

Agnew, Robert, and David M. Petersen. 1989. "Leisure and Delinquency." *Social Problems* 36, no. 4: 332–50.

Akers, Michelle. 1999. "A Welcome Timeout." *Sports Illustrated for Women* (Fall), 96–7.

Alley, Robert S. 1977. *Television: Ethics for Hire?* Nashville: Abingdon.

Allison, Lincoln. 1994. "The Olympic Movement and the End of the Cold War." *World Affairs* 157, no. 2: 92–7.

Alsop, Ronald. 1999a. "But Brewers Employ In-Your-Mug Approach." *Wall Street Journal* (29 June), B1.

———. 1999b. "Cracking the Gay Market Code." *Wall Street Journal* (29 June), B1, B4.

———. 1999c. "Are Gay People More Affluent Than Others?" *Wall Street Journal* (30 December), B1, B3.

Alter, Joseph S. 1995. "The Celibate Wrestler: Sexual Chaos, Embodied Balance and Competitive Politics in North India." *Contributions to Indian Sociology* 29, no. 1–2: 109–31.

"Amélie quería ser un hombre." 1999. *El Mundo* (7 March), n.p.

Anderson, Eric. 1999. "The Jock Closet." *xy Magazine*, no. 18 (April), 25–8.

Anderson, Kelly. 1999. "5 Easy Pieces." *Sports Illustrated for Women* (Fall), 84–5.

Andrews, David. 1993. "Desperately Seeking Michel: Foucault's Genealogy, the Body, and Critical Sport Sociology." *Sociology of Sport Journal* 10, no. 2: 148–67.

————, ed. 1996a. "Deconstructing Michael Jordan: Reconstructing Postindustrial America." *Sociology of Sport Journal* 13, no. 4: 315–467.

————. 1996b. "The Fact(s) of Michael Jordan's Blackness: Excavating a Floating Racial Signifier." *Sociology of Sport Journal* 13, no. 2: 125–58.

Andrews, David, Ben Carrington, Z. Mazur, and Steven J. Jackson. 1996. "Jordanscapes: A Preliminary Analysis of the Global Popular." *Sociology of Sport Journal* 13, no. 4: 428–57.

Andrews, Vernon L. 1996–97. "African American Player Codes on Celebration, Taunting, and Sportsmanlike Conduct." *Journal of African American Men* 2, no. 2–3: 57–92.

"Anger over Gay Taunts." 1999. *BBC News* (3 March). Available from: BBC Online Network.

Ann. 1993. "Rhonda's Book of Love Lines." *Sunday Times* (14 February), 6.

Araton, Henry. 1992. "Shameful: How Corporate America Dumped Magic." *Sydney Morning Herald* (2 January), 30.

————. 1999. "King Says Hingis Needs a Talking-To." *New York Times* (9 February), D1.

Arbena, Joseph L. 1993. "Sport and Social Change in Latin America." Pp. 97–117 in *Sport in Social Development: Traditions, Transitions, and Transformations*. Ed. Alan G. Ingham and John W. Loy. Champaign, Ill.: Human Kinetics Press.

"Are You a Victim of Runaway Fash?" 1998. *Sunday Mirror* (3 May), 8.

Armstrong, Gary. 1998. *Football Hooligans: Knowing the Score*. Oxford: Berg.

Athreya, Jayadev. 1998. "Pot or Not, Give Him Gold." *Iowa State Daily*, (13 February), n.p.

Atkin, R. 1999. "The Pride after the Prejudice." *Independent on Sunday* (7 February). 17.

Aycock, Alan. 1992. "The Confession of the Flesh: Disciplinary Gaze in Casual Bodybuilding." *Play and Culture* 5, no. 4: 338–57.

Badinter, Elisabeth. 1995. *XY: On Masculine Identity*. Trans. L. Davis. New York: Columbia University Press.

Bailey, Sandy. 1999. "From the Editor." *Sports Illustrated for Women* (Fall), 12.

Baker, Peter. 2000. "Once More with Feeling." *Future Talk*, 17–19.

Bale, John. 1991. *The Brawn Drain: Foreign Student–Athletes in American Universities*. Urbana: University of Illinois Press.

Bamberger, Michael, and Don Yaeger. 1997. "Over the Edge: Aware that Drug Testing Is a Sham, Athletes to Rely More than Ever on Banned Performance Enhancers." *Sports Illustrated* (14 April), 60–9.

Bank, David. 1999. "On the Web, Gay Sites Start to Click." *Wall Street Journal* (28 September), B1, B6.

Barak, G., ed. 1996. *Representing O. J.: Murder, Criminal Justice and Mass Culture*. New York: Harrow and Herston.

Barham, S. B. 1985. "The Phallus and the Man: An Analysis of Male Striptease." Pp. 51–65 in *Australian Ways: Anthropological Studies of an Industrialised Society*. Ed. Lenore Manderson. Sydney: Allen & Unwin.

Barratt, B. B., and B. R. Straus. 1994. "Toward Postmodern Masculinities." *American Imago* 51, no. 1: 37–67.

Bartky, Sarah L. 1988. "Foucault, Femininity, and the Modernisation of Patriarchal Power." *Feminism and Foucault: Reflections on Resistance*. Ed. I. Diamond and Lee Quimby. Boston: Northeastern University Press.

Begel, Daniel, and Antonia L. Baum. 2000. "The Athlete's Role." Pp. 45–58 in *Sport Psychiatry: Theory and Practice*. Ed. Daniel Begel and Robert W. Burton. New York: W. W. Norton.

Benaud, Richie. 1984. *Benaud on Reflection*. Sydney: Collins.

Benedict, Jeffrey R. 1998. *Athletes and Acquaintance Rape*. Thousand Oaks, Calif.: Sage.

"Ben Johnson to Take on Car, Horses in Charity Race." 1998. Web site. Available from: www.benjohnson979.com/news/charity_race.htm.

Benton, Ted. 1991. "Biology and Social Science: Why the Return of the Repressed Should Be Given a (Cautious) Welcome." *Sociology* 25, no. 1: 1–30.

Berkman, Andrew. 1999. "Trans-Gender Golf at Issue." *Women in Sport* 5, no. 4: 38–40.

Berkow, Ira. 1997. "Truth be Told, Louganis Must Be Free to Speak." *New York Times* (2 February), 7.

———. 1998. "Rodman Does the Unexpected." *New York Times* (30 May), C4.

Berlage, Gai I. 1992. "Women's Professional Baseball Gets a New Look: On Film and in Print." *Journal of Sport and Social Issues* 16, no. 2: 149–52.

Billings, Laura. 1999–2000. "Minnesota Vixens." *Sports Illustrated for Women* (Winter–Spring), 46–7.

Birrell, Susan, and Cheryl L. Cole. 1994. "Double Fault: Renee Richards and the Construction and Naturalization of Difference." Pp. 373–97 in *Women, Sport, and Culture*. Ed. Susan Birrell and Cheryl L. Cole. Champaign, Ill.: Human Kinetics Press.

Bledsoe, Lucy Jane. 1997. "Teamwork." Pp. 172–88 in *A Whole Other Ball Game: Women's Literature on Women's Sport*. Ed. Joli Sandoz. New York: Noonday Press.

Bletchley, Rachel. 1998a. "Gay Fash's Last Night of Lust." *Sun* (4 May), 6–7.

———. 1998b. "Shame of Fash." *Sun* (4 May), 1.

Blinde, Elaine M., and Diane E. Taub. 1992. "Women Athletes as Falsely Accused Deviants: Managing the Lesbian Stigma." *Sociological Quarterly* 33, no. 4: 521–33.

Blue, Adrianne. 1995. *Martina: The Lives and Times of Martina Navratilova.* New York: Birch Lane Press.

Boal, Mark. 1999. "Women are Easy." *Village Voice* (8 June), 40–2.

Bolin, Anne. 1992. "Flex Appeal, Food, and Fat: Competitive Bodybuilding, Gender, and Diet." *Play and Culture* 5, no. 4: 378–400.

Bordo, Susan. 1990. "Reading the Slender Body." In *Body/Politics: Women and the Discourses of Science.* Ed. M. Jacobus, E. Keller, and S. Shuttleworth. London: Routledge.

———. 1998. *The Male Body: A New Look at Men in Public and in Private.* New York: Farrar, Strauss & Giroux.

Boyd, Todd. 1997. "The Day the Niggaz Took Over: Basketball, Commodity Culture, and Black Masculinity." Pp. 123–42 in *Out of Bounds: Sports, Media, and the Politics of Identity.* Ed. Aaron Baker and Todd Boyd. Bloomington: Indiana University Press.

"Brady's Other Bunch." 1999. *Sports Illustrated* (16 August), 30.

"Breaking the Silence: Gays and Lesbians in Professional Sports." 1999. *New York Times* public forum (12 September). Available from: www.nytimes.com/sports.

Brodeur, Pierre. 1988. "Employee Fitness: Doctrines and Issues." Pp. 227–42 in *Not Just a Game: Essays in Canadian Sport Sociology.* Ed. Jean Harvey and Hart Cantelon. Ottawa: University of Ottawa Press.

Brown, Rita Mae. 1993. "Introduction." Pp. 11–22 in Sandra Faulkner with Judy Nelson, *Love Match: Nelson vs. Navratilova.* New York: Birch Lane Press.

Brownworth, V. A. 1994. "The Competitive Closet." Pp. 75–86 in *Sports-Dykes: Stories from On and Off the Field.* Ed. Susan Fox Rogers. New York: St. Martin's Press.

Bruce, Toni. 1998. "Audience Frustration and Pleasure: Women Viewers Confront Televised Women's Basketball." *Journal of Sport and Social Issues* 22, no. 4: 373–97.

Bryant, Jennings, Paul Comisky, and Dolf Zillmann. 1977. "Drama in Sports Commentary." *Journal of Communication* 26, no. 3: 140–9.

Budd, Joe. 1989. "A Tall Poppy Who Refuses to Bow." *Sunday Mail* (26 February), 1–2, 21.

Buffery, Steve. 1999a. "New Hurdle for Ben." *Toronto Sun* (20 July), 73.

———. 1999b. "Despite Ruling, Johnson Won't Go Quietly." *Toronto Sun* (17 August), 61.

Burfitt, John. 1996. "Twelve Months with Ian Roberts." *Outrage* (August), n.p.

Burke, Rose Marie. 1999. "Chippendales Let It All Hang Out in Europe." *Wall Street Journal* (8 April), A16.

Burroughs, A., L. Ashburn, and L. Seebohm. 1995. "'Add Sex and Stir': Homophobic Coverage of Women's Cricket in Australia." *Journal of Sport and Social Issues* 19, no. 3: 266–84.

Burstyn, Varda. 1999. *The Rites of Men: Manhood, Politics, and the Culture of Sport.* Toronto: University of Toronto Press.

Butler, Judith. 1998. "Athletic Genders: Hyperbolic Instance and/or the Overcoming of Sexual Binarism." *Stanford Humanities Review* 6, no. 2: 103–11.

Cagan, Joanna. 2000. "Objects of the Game." *Village Voice* (5 September), 182.

———. 1999. "The Second Sex and *SI* [*Sports Illustrated*]: Women Models Win Out over Women Writers." *Village Voice* (23 February), 173.

Cahill, P. 1997. "Pink Power's Diversity Carries Cash Clout." *Variety*, vol. 15–21 (September), 34, 44.

Cahn, Susan K. 1993. "From the 'Muscle Moll' to the 'Butch' Ballplayer: Mannishness, Lesbianism, and Homophobia in U.S. Women's Sport." *Feminist Studies* 19, no. 2: 343–68.

———. 1994. *Coming on Strong: Gender and Sexuality in Twentieth-Century Women's Sport.* Cambridge, Mass.: Harvard University Press.

Carlton, Mike. 1997. "Noine [*sic*] Hits a Bum Note." *Sydney Morning Herald* (7 June) 34.

Carmichael, Gordon A. 1992. "So Many Children: Colonial and Post-Colonial Demographic Patterns." Pp. 103–43 in *Gender Relations in Australia: Domination and Negotiation.* Ed. Kay Saunders and Raymond Evans. Sydney: Harcourt Brace Jovanovich.

Carroll, Susan J. 1999. "The Disempowerment of the Gender Gap: Soccer Moms and the 1996 Elections." *PS* 32, no. 1.

Cashman, Richard. 1995. *Paradise of Sport: The Rise of Organised Sport in Australia.* Melbourne: Oxford University Press.

"Catching Up with Tonya Butler." 1999–2000. *Sports Illustrated for Women* (Winter–Spring), 17.

Cawelti, John G. 1980. "Performance and Popular Culture." *Cinema Journal* 20, no. 1: 4–13.

Century, Douglas. 2000. "Women Mix It Up on TV with the X-and-0 Gang." *New York Times* (15 October), 1–2.

Chambers, Marcia. 1999. "Secret Videotapes Unnerve Athletes." *New York Times* (9 August), D4.

Champagne, John. 1996. "Homo Academicus." Pp. 49–79 in *Boys: Masculinities in Contemporary Culture.* Ed. Paul Smith. New York: Westview Press.

Chancer, L. 1998. "Playing Gender Against Race Through High-Profile Crime Cases: The Tyson/Thomas/Simpson Pattern of the 1980s." *Violence Against Women* 4: 100–13.

Chase, S. 1988. "Making Sense of 'The Woman Who Becomes a Man.'" In *Gender and Discourse: The Power of Talk*. Ed. A. Todd and S. Fisher. Norwood: Ablex.

Cherfils, Mildrade. 1999. "Police Arrest Rodman, Electra." Associated Press (5 November).

Chisholm, Ann. 1999. "Defending the Nation: National Bodies, U.S. Borders, and the 1996 U.S. Olympic Women's Gymnastics Team." *Journal of Sport and Social Issues* 23, no. 2: 126–39.

Clarey, C. 1999. "Unseeded Wonder Serves Davenport a Defeat." *International Herald Tribune* (29 January), n.p.

Clark, J. 1994. "Let the Games Begin." *Village Voice* (21 June), 12.

Clarke, Alan, and John Clarke. 1982. "Highlights and Action Replays— Ideology, Sport and the Media." Pp. 62–87 in *Sport, Culture and Ideology*. Ed. Jennifer Hargreaves. London: Routledge and Kegan Paul.

Coakley, Jay. 1999. "Interactive Review." *Quest* 51, no. 3: 285–9.

Cobb, Jean. 1993. "A Super Bowl–Battered Women Link?" *American Journalism Review* (May): 33–8.

Cole, Cheryl L. 1993. "Resisting the Canon: Feminist Cultural Studies, Sport, and Technologies of the Body." *Journal of Sport and Social Issues* 17, no. 2: 77–97.

Cole, C. L. 2000. "The Year That Girls Ruled." *Journal of Sport and Social Issues* 24, no. 1: 3–7.

Coleman, Wil. 1990. "Doing Masculinity/Doing Theory." Pp. 186–99 in *Men, Masculinities and Social Theory*. Ed. Jeff Hearn and David Morgan. London: Unwin Hyman.

Colombo, John Robert. 1994. "Ben Johnson 1988." *Colombo's All Time Great Canadian Quotations* (1 April). Self-published.

Colson, Bill. 1999. "Class of '99 Reunion." *Sports Illustrated* (20 December), 24.

Connell, R. W. 1987. *Gender and Power: Society, the Person, and Sexual Politics*. Cambridge: Polity Press.

———. 1990. "An Iron Man: The Body and Some Contradictions of Hegemonic Masculinity" In *Sport, Men, and the Gender Order: Critical Feminist Perspectives*. Ed. Michael A. Messner and Don Sabo. Champaign, Ill.: Human Kinetics Press.

———. 1992. "A Very Straight Gay: Masculinity, Homosexual Experience, and the Dynamics of Gender." *American Sociological Review* 57, no. 6: 735–51.

———. 1993. "The Big Picture: Masculinities in Recent World History." *Theory and Society* 22, no. 5: 597–623.

———. 1995. *Masculinities*. Berkeley: University of California Press.

———. 1996. "New Directions in Gender Theory, Masculinity Research, and Gender Politics." *Ethnos* 61, no. 3–4: 157–76.

———. 1998. "Masculinities and Globalization." *Men and Masculinities* 1, no. 1: 3–23.

Cooper, Pamela. 1995. "Marathon Women and the Corporation." *Journal of Women's History* 7, no. 4: 62–81.

Cox, Sue Mason, and Simone Fullagar. 1992. "The 'Feminine' in Sport." *Refractory Girl* 43: 21–4.

Crary, David. 1998. "Ten Years after Seoul, Ben Johnson Still Dreams of Comeback." Associated Press (18 September).

Creedon, Pamela J. 1998. "Women, Sport, and Media Institutions: Issues in Sports Journalism and Marketing." Pp. 88–99 in *MediaSport*. Ed. Lawrence A. Wenner. London: Routledge.

Crimp, Douglas. 1993. "Accommodating Magic." Pp. 254–66 in *Media Spectacles*. Ed. Marjorie Garber, Jann Matlock, and Rebecca Walkowitz. New York: Routledge.

Curran, Peggy. 1998. "Gay Games Ignored." *Montreal Gazette*, Internet edition (26 August). Available from: www.montrealgazette.com.

Curry, Timothy J. 1991. "Fraternal Bonding in the Locker Room: A Pro-feminist Analysis of Talk about Competition and Women." *Sociology of Sport Journal* 8, no. 2: 119–35.

Czoppelt, G. 1999. "Who Is Amelie Mauresmo?" Web site. Available from: hit.priv.at/maurem.

Daddario, G. 1997. "Gendered Sports Programming: 1992 Summer Olympic Coverage and the Feminine Narrative Form." *Sociology of Sport Journal* 14, no. 2: 103–20.

Daily Telegraph. 1996. Web site (27 July). Available from: www.mpx.com.au/~datam/1.html.

Davis, Kathy. 1997. "Was will der Mann?: Some Reflections on Theorizing Masculinity." *Theory and Psychology* 7, no. 4: 555–64.

Davis, Laurel R. 1997. *The Swimsuit Issue and Sport: Hegemonic Masculinity in* Sports Illustrated. Albany: State University of New York Press.

"Days of Their Lives." 1999. *Sports Illustrated for Women* (Fall), 95.

De Moragas Spà, M., N. K. Rivenbaugh, and J. F. Larson. 1995. *Television in the Olympics*. London: John Libbey.

Deacon, J. 1998. "Sex Sells—to a Point: While Katarina Witt Can Flaunt Her Sexuality, Many Gay Athletes Hide Theirs." *Maclean's* (30 November), 78.

Deford, Frank. 2000. "Advantage, Kournikova." *Sports Illustrated* (5 June), 94–108.

"Demo Derby." 1998. *Variety*, (8–14 June), 24.

Denizet-Lewis, Benoit. 1999. "The Last Closet." *xy*, no. 18 (April), 6.

Deutsher, Claire. 1999. "Image Is Everything, Isn't It?" *Women in Sport* 5, no. 4: 56–9.

Dewar, Alison. 1993. "Sexual Orientation in Sport: Past, Present, and Future Alternatives." Pp. 147–65 in *Sport in Social Development: Traditions, Transitions, and Transformations.* Ed. Alan G. Ingham and John W. Loy. Champaign, Ill.: Human Kinetics Press.

Dillman, L. 1999a. "Davenport Finally Meets Her Match." *Los Angeles Times* (28 January), 1.

———. 1999b. "Hingis Fires the First Volley." *Los Angeles Times* (29 January), 3.

———. 1999c. "Williams Sisters Find Solo Success." *Los Angeles Times* (1 March), D11.

Disch, Lisa, and Mary Jo Kane. 1996. "When a Looker Is Really a Bitch: Lisa Olson, Sport, and the Heterosexual Matrix." *Signs: Journal of Women in Culture and Society* 21, no. 2: 278–308.

Drape, Joe. 1999. "An Addict with One Weapon: Hope." *New York Times* (15 May), D1, D4.

Duncan, Margaret Carlisle. 1990. "Sports Photographs and Sexual Difference: Images of Women and Men in the 1984 and 1988 Olympic Games." *Sociology of Sport Journal* 7, no. 1: 22–42.

Duncan, Margaret Carlisle, and Michael A. Messner. 2000. "Gender in Televised Sports—Report to the Amateur Athletic Foundation of Los Angeles." Available from: www.aafla.org/publications/publications.htm.

———. 1998. "The Media Image of Sport and Gender." Pp. 170–85 in *MediaSport.* Ed. Lawrence A. Wenner. London: Routledge.

Dunne, S. 1997. "Local Hero." *Campaign,* no. 256 (July), 8–13, 48.

Duquin, Mary E. 1998. "The Swimsuit Issue and Sport as Critical Pedagogy." *International Review for the Sociology of Sport* 33, no. 2: 189–91.

Durie, John. 1992. "Safe Sex Eludes Rich and Famous." *Weekend Australian* (21–22 March), 10.

Dutter, B., and J. Parsons. 1999. "Muscular Lesbian Is a Very Nice Girl, Says Tennis No 1." *Daily Telegraph* (30 January), 4.

Dworkin, Shari Lee, and Faye Linda Wachs. 1998. "'Disciplining the Body': HIV-Positive Male Athletes, Media Surveillance, and the Policing of Sexuality." *Sociology of Sport Journal* 15, no. 1: 1–20.

Dyer, Richard. 1992. *Only Entertainment.* London: Routledge.

Dyson, Michael Eric. 1993. "Be Like Mike? Michael Jordan and the Pedagogy of Desire." *Cultural Studies* 7, no. 1: 64–72.

Early, Gerald. 1996. "Baseball, Boxing, and the Charisma of Sport and Race." Pp. 1–9 in *The Charisma of Sport and Race.* Doreen B. Townsend Centre for the Humanities Occasional Papers, no. 8.

Eastman, Susan Tyler, and Andrew C. Billings. 1999. "Gender Parity in the Olympics: Hyping Women Athletes, Favoring Men Athletes." *Journal of Sport and Social Issues* 23, no. 2: 140–70.

Eastman, Susan Tyler, and Arthur M. Land. 1997. "The Best of Both Worlds: Sports Fans Find Good Seats at the Bar." *Journal of Sport and Social Issues* 21, no. 2: 156–78.

Eco, Umberto. 1987 [1969]. *Travels in Hyperreality: Essays,* repr. ed. Trans. William Weaver. London: Picador.

Edgerton, Gary, and David Ostroff. 1985. "Sports Telecasting." Pp. 257–86 in *TV Genres: A Handbook and Reference Guide.* Ed. Brian G. Rose. Westport, Conn.: Greenwood Press.

Eichberg, Henning. 1986. "The Enclosure of the Body—On the Historical Relativity of 'Health,' 'Nature' and the Environment of Sport." *Journal of Contemporary History* 21, no. 1: 99–121.

Eitzen, D. Stanley. 1999. *Fair and Foul: Beyond the Myths and Paradoxes of Sport.* Lanham, Md.: Rowman & Littlefield.

Elias, Norbert. 1986a. "An Essay on Sport and Violence." Pp. 150–74 in Norbert Elias and Eric Dunning, *Quest for Excitement: Sport and Leisure in the Civilizing Process.* Oxford: Basil Blackwell.

———. 1986b. "Introduction." Pp. 19–62 in Norbert Elias and Eric Dunning, *Quest for Excitement: Sport and Leisure in the Civilizing Process.* Oxford: Basil Blackwell.

Elliott, S. 1998a. "Levi Strauss Begins a Far-Reaching Marketing Campaign to Reach Gay Men and Lesbians." *New York Times* (19 October), C11.

———. 1998b. "TV Sports Lose Some of Their Power to Reach America's Men." *New York Times* (26 October), C1, 9.

Ellsworth, Elizabeth. 1986. "Illicit Pleasures: Feminist Spectators and *Personal Best." Wide Angle* 8, no. 2: 45–56.

Elson, J. 1991. "The Dangerous World of Wannabes." *Time* (25 November), 59–60.

Embrey, Lynn, Anne Hall, and Anne Gunter. 1992. "Olympians Facing the Media." *Refractory Girl* 43: 10–13.

Evans, L. 1998. "Kournikova Has Eyes Only for the Lead Role and Center Stage." *Sydney Morning Herald* (10 January), 10.

Falk, Pasi. 1994. *The Consuming Body.* London: Sage.

Farber, Michael. 1996. "The World/Track and Field: Blast from the North." *Sports Illustrated* (22 July), 22–27.

Farred, Grant. 1996. "The Prettiest Postcolonial: Muhammad Ali." Pp. 151–70 in *Boys: Masculinities in Contemporary Culture.* Ed. Paul Smith. New York: Westview Press.

Featherstone, Mike, Mike Hepworth, and Bryan Turner, eds. 1991. *The Body: Social Processes and Social Theory*. London: Sage.

Feder, Abigail. 1994. "Kiss Me, Skate." *Village Voice* (5 July), 140.

Fiddes, Nick. 1991. *Meat: A Natural Symbol*. London: Routledge.

Fish, Mike. 1998. "Sexual Orientation Issue Lurks under Surface in Women's Athletics." *Milwaukee Journal Sentinel* (27 September), 12–18.

Flaherty, George. 1999. "Confessions of a Muscle Queen." *xy Magazine*, no. 18 (April), 18–20.

Flannery, T. 1996. "Sports and the Courts: Several Issues Should be Considered Before Starting Drug-Testing Program." *Interscholastic Athletic Administration* 22, no. 3: 8–12.

Fornoff, Susan. 1993. *"Lady in the Locker Room": Uncovering the Oakland Athletics*. Champaign, Ill.: Sagamore Press.

Foss, Paul. 1985. "Mapplethorpe Aglance." *Photofile* 3, no. 3: 8–10.

Foucault, Michel. 1986. *The Use of Pleasure: The History of Sexuality, Volume Two*. Trans. Robert Hurley. New York: Vintage.

———. 1988. *The Care of the Self: The History of Sexuality, Volume 3*. Trans. Robert Hurley. New York: Vintage.

Fox, C. 1989. "Decade of the 'New Man' Is Here." *Australian Financial Review* (21 January), 46.

Frank, Arthur. 1991. "For a Sociology of the Body: An Analytical Review." In *The Body: Social Processes and Social Theory*. Ed. Mike Featherstone, Mike Hepworth, and Bryan Turner. London: Sage.

Freeman, Paul. 1997. *Ian Roberts: Finding Out*. Sydney: Random House.

Freudenheim, Milt. 1999. "Employers Focus on Weight as Workplace Health Issue." *New York Times* (6 September), A15.

Frey, J. 1994. "A Boy of Summer's Long, Chilly Winter; Once a Promising Ballplayer, Glenn Burke Is Dying of AIDS." *New York Times* (18 October), B15.

Fusco, Carolyn. 1998. "Lesbians and Locker Rooms: The Subjective Experiences of Lesbians in Sport." Pp. 87–116 in *Sport and Postmodern Times*. Ed. Geneviève Rail. Albany: State University of New York Press.

Fussell, Sam. 1993. "Bodybuilder Americanus." *Michigan Quarterly Review* 32, no. 4: 577–96.

Galst, Liz. 1998. "The Sports Closet." *Ms* (September–October), n.p.

Galvin, P. 1997. "Dennis the Menace." *The Advocate*, no. 724–25 (21 January), 26–34.

Gatens, Moira. 1988. "Towards a Feminist Philosophy of the Body." In *Crossing Boundaries*. Ed. Barbara Caine, Elizabeth Grosz, and Marie de Lepervanche. Sydney: Allen & Unwin.

Gatt, Ray. 1998. "Anna Has Her Wicket Way with Warne." *Australian* (14 January), 5.

"Gay Plagued League Star." 1998. *The Press* (9 November), PSA-2220.

"Gays and the Australian Economy" 1999. *The Economist* (11 December), n.p. Available from: people.smartchat.net.au/~tonywhelan/gaysport/profiles/ian_roberts.htm

Geurens, Jean-Pierre. 1989. "The Brainbusters: The Upside Down World of Television Wrestling." *Spectator,* vol. 9, no. 2, 56–67.

Gibson, Althea. 1979. "I Always Wanted to Be Somebody." Pp. 130–42 in *Out of the Bleachers: Writings on Women and Sport.* Ed. S. L. Twin. New York: Feminist Press/McGraw-Hill.

Girard, René. 1992. *Violence and the Sacred.* Trans. P. Gregory. Baltimore: Johns Hopkins University Press.

"The Girls of Summer." 1999. *Wall Street Journal* (13 July), A22.

Gledhill, Christine. 1991. "Introduction." Pp. xiii–xx in *Stardom: Industry of Desire.* Ed. Christine Gledhill. London: Routledge.

GLINN. N.d. *Gay Sports News.*

Gluckman, Amy, and Betsy Reed, eds. 1997. *Homo Economics: Capitalism, Community, and Lesbian and Gay Life.* New York: Routledge.

Gmelch, George, and Patricia M. San Antonio. 1998. "Groupies and American Baseball." *Journal of Sport and Social Issues* 22, no. 1: 32–45.

"Go Figure." 1999. *Sports Illustrated for Women* (Fall), 20.

"Go Figure." 1999–2000. *Sports Illustrated for Women* (Winter–Spring), 22.

"Gorgeous Women of Tennis." 1999. *Women in Sport* 5, no. 4: 79.

Goss, G. 1943. "Tennis." Pp. 308–52 in *Individual Sports for Women.* Ed. D. S. Ainsworth, M. R. Broer, A. G. Goss, G. Goss, E. Jennings, B. A. Pitkin, and F. Ryder. Philadelphia: W. B. Saunders.

"Grace v. Power: An Eternal Struggle." 1999. *Sydney Morning Herald* (30 January), 50.

Gramsci, Antonio. 1978. *Selections from the Prison Notebooks of Antonio Gramsci.* Trans. and ed. Quentin Hoare and Geoffrey Nowell-Smith. New York: International Publishers.

Griffin, Christine. 1993. *Representations of Youth: The Study of Youth and Adolescence in Britain and America.* Cambridge: Polity Press.

Griffin, Pat. 1998. *Strong Women, Deep Closets: Lesbians and Homophobia in Sport.* Champaign, Ill.: Human Kinetics Press.

Gross, George. 1999. "Big Ben's Blackballed." *Calgary Sun* (21 August), F8.

Gross, Larry. 1991. "The Contested Closet: The Ethics and Politics of Outing." *Critical Studies in Mass Communication* 8, no. 3: 352–88.

Grosz, Elizabeth. 1987. "Notes Towards a Corporeal Feminism." *Australian Feminist Studies* 5: 1–16.

"Group to Study Johnson's Bid." 1999. *New York Times* (20 May), D7.

Gruneau, Richard. 1991. "Sport and 'Esprit de Corps': Notes on Power, Culture and the Politics of the Body." In *Sport: The Third Millennium*. Ed. F. Landry, M. Landry, and M. Yerles. Laval: Les Presses de L'Université Laval.

———. 1993. "The Critique of Sport in Modernity: Theorising Power, Culture, and the Politics of the Body." Pp. 85–109 in *The Sports Process: A Comparative and Developmental Approach*. Ed. Eric Dunning, Joseph A. Maguire, and Robert E. Pearton. Champaign, Ill.: Human Kinetics Press.

Gruneau, Richard, and David Whitson. 1993. *Hockey Night in Canada: Sport, Identities and Cultural Politics*. Toronto: Garamond Press.

Guthrie, Sharon, and Shirley Castelnuovo. 1999. "Interactive Review." *Quest* 51, no. 3: 289–301.

Guttmann, Allen. 1994. *Games and Empires: Modern Sports and Cultural Imperialism*. New York: Columbia University Press. .

Halbert, Christy. 1997. "Tough Enough and Woman Enough: Stereotypes, Discrimination, and Impression Management among Women Professional Boxers." *Journal of Sport and Social Issues* 21, no. 1: 7–36.

Halberstam, Judith. 1998. *Female Masculinity*. Durham, N.C.: Duke University Press.

Hall, M. Ann. 1993. "Gender and Sport in the 1990s: Feminism, Culture, and Politics." *Sport Science Review* 2, no. 1: 48–68.

———. 1995. "Feminist Activism in Sport: A Comparative Study of Women's Sport Advocacy Organizations." Pp. 217–50 in *Gender, Sport and Leisure: Continuities and Challenges*. Ed. Alan Tomlinson. Aachen: Meyer & Meyer Verlag.

———. 1996. *Feminism and Sporting Bodies: Essays on Theory and Practice*. Champaign, Ill.: Human Kinetics Press.

———. 1999. "Boxers and Bodymakers: Third-Wave Feminism and the Remaking of Women's Sport." Paper presented at Dimensionen und Visionen des Sports Conference, Heidelberg, 27–29 September.

Hall, Stephen S. 1999. "The Bully in the Mirror." *New York Times Magazine* (22 August), 30–5, 58–65.

Hall, Stuart. 1981. "Notes on Deconstructing 'The Popular.'" In *People's History and Socialist Theory*. Ed. Raphael Samuel. London: Routledge and Kegan Paul.

———. 1991. "Old and New Identities, Old and New Ethnicities." Pp. 41–68 in *Culture, Globalization and the World-System: Contemporary Conditions for the Representation of Identity*. Ed. Anthony D. King. London: Macmillan.

———. 1997. "The Spectacle of the 'Other.'" Pp. 223–79 in *Representation: Cultural Representations and Signifying Practices*. Ed. Stuart Hall. London: Sage.

Hamermesh, D. S., and J. E. Biddle. 1994. "Beauty and the Labor Market." *American Economic Review* 84, no. 5: 1174–94.

Hamilton, William L. 2000. "When Intentions Fall Between the Lines." *New York Times* (20 July), F1, F4.

Hanlon, Peter. 1998. "Loneliness of the Gay Footballer." *Sunday Age* (10 May).

Harari, Fiona. 1993. "The New Face of Beauty." *Australian* (18 June), 15.

Hargreaves, Jennifer. 1994. *Sporting Females: Critical Issues in the History and Sociology of Women's Sports.* London: Routledge.

Hargreaves, John. 1986. *Sport, Power and Culture.* Cambridge: Polity Press.

Harper, Phillip Brian. 1996. *Are We Not Men? Masculine Anxiety and the Problem of African-American Identity.* New York: Oxford University Press.

Hearn, Jeff. 1992. *Men in the Public Eye: The Construction and Deconstruction of Public Men and Public Patriarchies.* London: Routledge.

Heikkala, J. 1993. "Discipline and Excel: Techniques of Self and Body and the Logic of Competing." *Sociology of Sport Journal* 10, no. 4: 397–412.

"Help Offered to Suicidal Young." 1999. *Sydney Morning Herald* Internet edition (4 May). Available from: www.smh.com.au/news/990504/national/national13.html.

Heuring, David. 1988. "Live Sports Broadcasts Require Quick Eyes." *American Cinematographer,* vol. 64, no. 10, 86–94.

Heywood, Leslie. 2000. *Pretty Good for a Girl: An Athlete's Story.* Minneapolis: University of Minnesota Press.

Higgs, C. T., and K. H. Weiller. 1994. "Gender Bias and the 1992 Summer Olympic Games: An Analysis of Television Coverage." *Journal of Sport and Social Issues* 18, no. 3: 234–46.

"Hingis Prevails in Grudge Match: Kafelnikov Falters." 1999. *Washington Times* (27 May), B6.

Hitchcock, John R. 1991. *Sportscasting.* Boston: Focal Press.

"Hockey Teams' Bad Dreams." 1991. *Sydney Morning Herald* (6 December), 7.

Hogan, J. 1998. "Kournikova Plays Waiting Game." *Australian* (14 January), 50.

Hoggart, Richard. 1971. *The Uses of Literacy: Aspects of Working-Class Life with Special Reference to Publications and Entertainments.* Harmondsworth: Penguin.

Hole, J. 1992. "Outrage as Basketballers Shun Magic." *Sydney Morning Herald* (25 January), 1–2.

Hornung, E. W. 1936. *Raffles: The Amateur Cracksman.* London: Jonathan Cape.

Horrocks, Roger. 1995. *Male Myths and Icons: Masculinity in Popular Culture*. New York: St. Martin's Press.

Houlihan, Barrie. 1994. *Sport and International Politics*. London: Harvester Wheatsheaf.

"Hugh, Idiot." 1999. *Sports Illustrated* (August), 36.

Hunt, Paula. 2000. "They Don't Skate Straight." *Village Voice* (29 February), 166.

Huxley, J. 1989. "Alive and Kicking." *Sydney Morning Herald* (23 September), 76.

"Ian Roberts Fabulous Footballer." N.d. Website. Available from: Gay.Net.

Ian Roberts Tribute Page. N.d. Website. Available from: www.timbomb.net/ian/text.html.

"Irresponsible Athletes." 1998. *New York Times* (6 May), A22.

Jackson, Steven J. 1998a. "A Twist of Race: Ben Johnson and the Canadian Crisis of Racial and National Identity." *Sociology of Sport Journal* 15, no. 1: 21–40.

———. 1998b. "Life in the (Mediated) Faust Lane: Ben Johnson, National Affect and the 1988 Crisis of Canadian Identity." *International Review for the Sociology of Sport* 33: 227–38.

Jackson, Steven J., David Andrews, and Cheryl L. Cole. 1998. "Race, Nation and Authenticity of Identity: Interrogating the 'Everywhere' Man (Michael Jordan) and the 'Nowhere' Man (Ben Johnson)." *Journal of Immigrants and Minorities* 17, no. 1: 82–102.

Jarvie, Grant, and Joseph Maguire. 1994. *Sport and Leisure in Social Thought*. London: Routledge.

Jefferson Lenskyj, Helen. 1998. "'Inside Sport' or 'On the Margins'? Australian Women and the Sport Media." *International Review for the Sociology of Sport* 33, no. 1: 19–32.

Jefferson, T. 1997. "The Tyson Rape Trial: The Law, Feminism and Emotional 'Truth.'" *Social and Legal Studies* 6: 281–301.

———. 1998. "On Muscle, Hard Men, and Iron Mike Tyson: Reflections on Desire, Anxiety and the Embodiment of Masculinity." *Body and Society* 4, no. 2: 77–98.

Jenkins, Emily. 1998. *Tongue First: Adventures in Physical Culture*. New York: Henry Holt.

Jiobu, Robert M. 1988. "Racial Inequality in a Public Arena: The Case of Baseball." *Social Forces* 67, no. 2: 524–34.

"Johnson Demeans Blacks by Racing a Horse." 1998. *Toronto Star* (8 October).

Johnson, Earvin, and Johnson, Roy. 1991. "I'll Deal with It." *Sports Illustrated* (18 November), 22.

"Johnson Fails Another Test." 1999. *New York Times* (16 November), D7.

"Johnson's Appeal Denied; Sotomayor Facing Ban." 1999. *New York Times* (17 August), D2.

"Johnson Wants to Run Again." 1996. Reuters (20 November).

Kane, Mary Jo, and Helen Jefferson Lenskyj. 1998. "Media Treatment of Female Athletes: Issues of Gender and Sexualities." Pp. 187–201 in *MediaSport*. Ed. Lawrence A. Wenner. London: Routledge.

Kang, Joon-Mann. 1988. "Sports, Media and Cultural Dependency." *Journal of Contemporary Asia* 18, no. 4: 430–43.

Kimmel, Michael S. 1992. "Reading Men: Men, Masculinity, and Publishing." *Contemporary Sociology* 21, no. 2: 162–71.

———. 1995. "Clarence, William, Iron Mike, Tailhook, Senator Packwood ... and Us." *Men's Lives*, 3rd ed. Ed. Michael S. Kimmel and Michael A. Messsner. Boston: Allyn and Bacon.

King, Barry. 1987. "The Star and the Commodity: Notes Towards a Performance Theory of Stardom." *Cultural Studies* 1, no. 2: 145–61.

King, Kelley. 1999. "A Big Hit Little Cities." *Sports Illustrated* (6 September), n.p.

King, S. 1993. "The Politics of the Body and the Body Politic: Magic Johnson and the Ideology of AIDS." *Sociology of Sport Journal* 10, no. 3: 270–85.

Kingston, Geoff. 1990. "Games Commentator Shut Out." *Weekend Australian* (27–28 January), 3.

Kinnick, Katherine N. 1998. "Gender Bias in Newspaper Profiles of 1996 Olympic Athletes: A Content Analysis of Five Major Dailies." *Women's Studies in Communication* 21, no. 2: 212–37.

Kirby, Stephen. 1986. "The Lure of the Locker Room." *Outrage*, no. 40 (September), 15.

Kirk, David, ed. 1993. *The Body, Schooling and Culture: A Reader.* Geelong, Australia: Deakin University Press.

Klein, Alan M. 1995. "Life's Too Short to Die Small: Steroid Use among Male Bodybuilders." Pp. 105–20 in *Men's Health and Illness: Gender, Power, and the Body*. Ed. Donald Sabo and David Frederick Gordon. Thousand Oaks, Calif.: Sage.

Knitting Circle. n.d. E-mail listserv. Available from: stafflag@sbu.ac.uk.

Kort, Michelle. 1994. "Interview: Martina Navratilova." Pp. 133–42 in *SportsDykes: Stories from On and Off the Field*. Ed. Susan Fox Rogers. New York: St. Martin's Press.

Krane, V., and L. Romont. 1997. "Female Athletes' Motives and Experiences during the Gay Games." *Journal of Gay, Lesbian, and Bisexual Identity* 2, no. 2: 123–38.

Kroker, Arthur, M. Kroker, and D. Cook. 1989. *Panic Encyclopedia: The Definitive Guide to the Postmodern Scene.* London: Macmillan.

Lafrance, Mélisse, and Geneviève Rail. 2000. "'As Bad as He Says He Is?' Interrogating Dennis Rodman's Subversive Potential." Pp. 74–107 in *Reading Sport: Critical Essays on Power and Representation.* Ed. Susan Birrell and Mary G. McDonald. Boston: Northeastern University Press.

Lapchick, Richard E., and Jeffrey R. Benedict. 1993. "Racial Report Card." *CSSS Digest* 5, no. 1: 1, 4–8, 12–3.

Lapchick, Richard E., with Kevin J. Matthews. N.d. *1997 Racial Report Card.* Center for the Study of Sport in Society, Northeastern University.

Lasch, Christopher. 1979. *The Culture of Narcissism: American Life in an Age of Diminishing Expectations.* New York: Warner.

"Laurie Lawrence Profile." N.d. Available from: www.hpo.com.au/profile/laurielawrence.htm.

Layden, Tim. 1999a. "Bare Naked Lady." *Sports Illustrated for Women* (Fall), 110–11.

———. 1999b. "Coming Out Party." *Sports Illustrated* (8 February), 58.

Leader, Zachary. 1999. "Diving to Make a Point." *Times Literary Supplement* (23 July), 6.

Leand, Andrea. 1999. "French Teen Bursts onto Scene: Mauresmo Credits Her Girlfriend for Success." *USA Today* (29 January), 3C.

Leand, Andrea, and Doug Smith. 1999. "Hingis Cool under Fire." *USA Today* (27 May), 16C.

Leath, Virginia M., and Angela Lumpkin. 1992. "An Analysis of Sportswomen on the Covers and in the Feature Articles of Women's Sports and Fitness Magazine, 1975–1989." *Journal of Sport and Social Issues* 16, no. 2: 121–6.

Lemon, B. 1997a. "Male Beauty." *The Advocate,* no. 738 (22 July): 30–2.

———. 1997b. "Mr. USA Is Gay!" *The Advocate,* no. 738 (22 July), 26–9.

Lenskyj, Helen. 1986. *Out of Bounds: Women, Sport and Sexuality.* Toronto: Women's Press.

———. 1991. "Combating Homophobia in Sport and Physical Education." *Sociology of Sport Journal* 8, no. 1: 61–9.

Lewis, P. 1985. "Men on Pedestals." *Ten-8,* no. 17, 22–9.

Lichtenstein, G. 1998. "Net Profits." Pp. 57–77 in *Nike Is a Goddess: The History of Women in Sports.* Ed. L. Smith. New York: Atlantic Monthly Press.

Lipsyte, Robert. 1991. "Gay Bias Moves Off the Sidelines." *New York Times* (24 May), B11.

———. 1997. "For Gays in Team Sports, Still a Deafening Silence." *New York Times* (7 September), S15.

———. 1999a. "Sports and Sex Are Always Together." *New York Times* (11 July), 13.

———. 1999b. "O.K., Sports Isn't Solely About Sex." *New York Times* (18 July), 13.

———. 1999c. "A Major League Player's Life of Isolation and Subterfuge." *New York Times* (6 September), A1, D8.

———. 1999d. "Reflections on a Secret Life in Professional Sports." *New York Times* (12 September), 3.

Longman, Jere. 2000. "Women Move Closer to Olympic Equality." *New York Times* (20 August), 1, 24.

———. 1999a. "Pride in Their Play, and in Their Bodies." *New York Times* (8 July), D1, D4.

———. 1999b. "Heinrichs in Running to Coach U.S. Women's Olympians." *New York Times* (18 December), D2.

———. 2000. "Heinrichs to Be Coach of U.S. Women's Team." *New York Times* (17 January), D7.

Lopiano, Donna A. 1998. "Foreword." Pp. vii–viii in Pat Griffin, *Strong Women, Deep Closets: Lesbians and Homophobia in Sport*. Champaign, Ill.: Human Kinetics Press.

Loy, John, David L. Andrews, and Robert E. Rinehart. 1993. "The Body in Culture and Sport." *Sport Science Review* 2, no. 1: 69–91.

Lueschen, Guenther. 1993. "Doping in Sport: The Social Structure of a Deviant Subculture." *Sport Science Review* 2, no. 1: 92–106.

Lule, J. 1995. "The Rape of Mike Tyson: Race, the Press and Symbolic Types." *Critical Studies in Mass Communication* 12, no. 3: 176–95.

Lumpkin, Angela, and Linda D. Williams. 1991. "An Analysis of *Sports Illustrated* Feature Articles, 1954–1987." *Sociology of Sport Journal* 8, no. 1: 16–32.

Lurie, Rachel. 1994. "Martina and Me: A Trilogy." Pp. 120–9 in *Sports-Dykes: Stories from On and Off the Field*. Ed. Susan Fox Rogers. New York: St. Martin's Press.

Lusetich, R. 1999. "Girls Take Giant Step for Womankind." *Weekend Australian* (17–18 July), 53.

Lynch, M., and L. May. 1989. "Tina's Turn One Leg of the Fight for Fans." *Australian Financial Review* (21 March), 50.

Lynd, Robert S., and Helen Merrell Lynd. 1956. *Middletown: A Study in Modern American Culture*. New York: Harcourt, Brace and Company.

———. 1965. *Middletown in Transition: A Study in Cultural Conflicts*. New York: Harcourt Brace Jovanovich.

MacDonald, J. 1998. "Fairer Sex Has Only S and V to Play With." *Australian* (14 January), 18.

Macdonald, M. 1997. *Representing Women: Myths of Femininity in the Popular Media*. London: Arnold.

Magic Johnson Foundation. N.d. Available from: www.magicjohnson.org.

"Magic Makes Comeback with LA Lakers." 1996. *Jet* (19 February), 52.

"'Man' Taunts Fire Up Mauresmo ... Mauresmo Out in the Open." 1999. *Weekend Australian* (30–31 January), 63, 5.

Marchese, John. 1993. "Bustin' Stereotypes." *New York Times* (26 September), 8v.

"Marketplace." 1999. National Public Radio (3 June).

Mariscal, Jorge. 1999. "Chicanos and Latinos in the Jungle of Sports Talk Radio." *Journal of Sport and Social Issues* 23, no. 1: 111–17.

Markula, Pirkko. 1999. "Review." *Sociology of Sport Journal* 16, no. 2: 174–6.

Marquesee, Mike. 1994. *Anyone but England: Cricket and the National Malaise*. London: Verso.

Martin, Lydia. 1999. "Ex-Ballplayer Finds Freedom in Truth." *Miami Herald* (9 August), 4C.

Marshall, D. W., and G. Cook. 1992. "The Corporate (Sports) Sponsor." *International Journal of Advertising* 11, no. 4: 307–24.

Mass-Observation. 1939. *Britain*. Harmondsworth: Penguin.

Mazer, Sharon. 1998. *Professional Wrestling: Sport and Spectacle*. Jackson: University Press of Mississippi.

McCarthy, Anna. 1995. "'The Front Row Is Reserved for Scotch Drinkers': Early Television's Tavern Audiences." *Cinema Journal* 34, no. 4: 31–49.

McDowell, Dimity. 1999–2000a. "Au Naturel Athlete." *Sports Illustrated for Women* (Winter–Spring), 20.

———. "Wonder Women." 1999–2000b. *Sports Illustrated for Women* (Winter–Spring), 94–8.

McGinn, Colin. 1999. "The Hollow Man's Story." *Times Literary Supplement* (25 June), 3.

McHoul, Alec. 1997. "On Doing 'We's': Where Sport Leaks into Everyday Life." *Journal of Sport and Social Issues* 21, no. 3: 315–20.

McKay, Jim. 1991. *No Pain, No Gain? Sport and Australian Culture*. Sydney: Prentice Hall.

———. 1992. "Sport and the Social Construction of Gender." Pp. 245–65 in *Society and Gender: An Introduction to Sociology*. Ed. Gillian Lupton, Patricia M. Short, and Rosemary Whip. Sydney: Macmillan.

———. 1993. "'Marked Men' and 'Wanton Women': The Politics of Naming Sexual 'Deviance' in Sport." *Journal of Men's Studies* 2: 69–87.

———. 1995. "'Just Do It': Corporate Sports Slogans and the Political Economy of 'Enlightened Racism.'" *Discourse: Studies in the Cultural Politics of Education* 16, no. 2: 191–201.

———. 1997. *Managing Gender: Affirmative Action and Organizational Power in Australian, Canadian, and New Zealand Sport*. Albany: State University of New York Press.

McKay, Jim, and Debbie Huber. 1992. "Anchoring Media Images of Technology and Sport." *Women's Studies International Forum* 15, no. 2: 205–18.

McKay, Jim, and Philip Smith. 1995. "Exonerating the Hero: Frames and Narratives in Media Coverage of the O. J. Simpson Story." *Media Information Australia*, no. 75 (February), 57–66.

McMurtry, Roy. 1993. "Sport and the Commonwealth Heads of Government." *Round Table* 328: 414–26.

Mead, Rebecca. 1999. "Exposure." *New Yorker* (26 July), 25.

Mercer, Kobena, and Isaac Julien. 1992. "True Confessions: A Discourse on Images of Black Male Sexuality." *Ten-8*, vol. 2, no. 3, 40–9.

Messner, Michael A. 1988. "Sports and Male Domination: The Female Athlete as Contested Terrain." *Sociology of Sport Journal* 5: 197–211.

———. 1990. "When Bodies Are Weapons: Masculinity and Violence in Sport." *International Review for the Sociology of Sport* 25: 203–19.

———. 1997. *Politics of Masculinities: Men in Movements.* Thousand Oaks, Calif.: Sage.

Messner, Michael A., Margaret Carlisle Duncan, and Kerry Jensen. 1993. "Separating the Men from the Girls: The Gendered Language of Televised Sports." *Gender and Society* 7, no. 1: 121–37.

Messner, Michael A., and W. Solomon. 1993. "Outside the Frame: Newspaper Coverage of the Sugar Ray Leonard Wife Abuse Story." *Sociology of Sport Journal* 10: 119–34.

Mikosza, J., and M. Phillips. 1999. "Gender, Sport and the Body Politic: The Framing of Femininity in the *Golden Girls of Sport Calendar* and *The Atlanta Dream.*" *International Review for the Sociology of Sport* 34, no. 1: 5–16.

Millar, Damien. 1997. "Hard Copy." *Campaign*, no. 256 (July), 56.

Miller, D. A. 1992. "Bringing out Roland Barthes." *Raritan*, vol. 11, no. 4, 38–49.

Miller, D. M., and K. L. Ley. 1956. *Individual and Team Sports for Women.* Englewood Cliffs, N.J.: Prentice-Hall.

Miller, Russell. 1992. "Can Tyson Beat the Rape Rap?" *Weekend Australian Review* (5–6 September), 3.

Miller, Toby. 1989. "World Series Sound and Vision." *Meanjin* 48, no. 3: 591–6.

———. 1990. "Sport, Media and Masculinity." Pp. 74–95 in *Sport and Leisure: Trends in Australian Popular Culture.* Ed. David Rowe and Geoffrey Lawrence. Orlando, Fla.: Harcourt Brace.

———. 1998. *Technologies of Truth: Cultural Citizenship and the Popular Media.* Minneapolis: University of Minnesota Press.

Mitchell, Susan, and Ken Dyer. 1985. *Winning Women: Challenging the Norms in Australian Sport.* Ringwood, Va.: Penguin.

Monnington, Terry. 1993. "Politicians and Sport: Uses and Abuses." Pp. 125–50 in *The Changing Politics of Sport.* Ed. Lincoln Allison. Manchester: Manchester University Press.

Morris, Barbara, and Joel Nydahl. 1985. "Sports Spectacle as Drama: Image, Language, and Technology." *Journal of Popular Culture* 18, no. 4: 101–10.

Morrison, Toni. 1997. "The Official Story: Dead Man Golfing—Introduction." Pp. vii–xxviii in *Birth of a Nation'hood: Gaze, Script, and Spectacle in the O. J. Simpson Case.* Ed. Toni Morrison and Claudia Brodsky Lacour. New York: Pantheon.

Morse, Margaret. 1983. "Sport on Television: Replay and Display." Pp. 44–66 in *Regarding Television.* Ed. E. Ann Kaplan. Los Angeles: American Film Institute.

Moss, Howard B., George L. Panzak, and Ralph E. Tarter. 1993. "Sexual Functioning of Male Anabolic Steroid Users." *Archives of Sexual Behavior* 22, no. 1: 1–12.

Murphy, F. N.d. "Laurie Lawrence's All-Time Top 10." Australian Swimming and Fitness Web site. Available from: www.magna.com.au/~iphala/sf_sweat.htm.

Nack, William, and Don Yaeger. 1999. "Who's Coaching Your Kid? Every Parent's Nightmare." *Sports Illustrated* (13 September), 40–53.

"The Naked Truth." 2000. *Sports Illustrated* (11 September), 36.

Name withheld by request. 1997. "The Whole Nine Yards." *The Advocate,* no. 726 (4 February), 6.

Nationwide Realty National Convention. 1996. Web site. Available from: www.testra.com.au/pres/event/nationw/html/howe/hilites/speakers/lawrence.htm.

Naughton, P. 1999. "Davenport Asks: Who Is This Guy?" Reuters (28 January).

Navratilova, Martina, and Liz Nickles. 1996. *Breaking Point.* New York: Ballentine.

Navratilova, Martina, with George Vecsey. 1985. *Martina.* New York: Alfred A. Knopf.

Ndalianis, Angela. 1995. "Muscle, Excess and Rupture: Female Bodybuilding and Gender Construction." *Media Information Australia* (February), 13–23.

Nelson, Mariah Burton. 1994. "Personal Focus." *Gay Games IV Official Souvenir Program,* 34–5.

———. 1999. "Learning What 'Team' Really Means." *Newsweek* (19 July), 55.

Newkey-Burden, Chas. 1998. "All Lads Together?" *Attitude* 1, no. 51: 92–4.

Nittve, L. 1987. *Implosion: A Postmodern Perspective.* Stockholm: Moderna Museet.

Nixon, Sean. 1996. *Hard Looks: Masculinities, Spectatorship and Contemporary Consumption.* New York: St. Martin's Press.

"No. 1 Hingis Needs Leadership Skills." 1999. *Miami Herald* Internet edition (11 February). Available from: www.herald.com.

O'Connor, J. J. 1997. "Coming Out Party: The Closet Opens, Finally." *New York Times* (30 April), C18.

O'Donnell, Hugh. 1994. "Mapping the Mythical: A Geopolitics of National Sporting Stereotypes." *Discourse and Society* 5, no. 3: 345–80.

"Oklahoma Crude." 1999. *Sports Illustrated* (1 November), 32–3.

Olney, Buster. 1999. "Bean's Friends and Former Teammates Give Him Their Unconditional Acceptance." *New York Times* (7 September), D3.

O'Neill, John. 1990. "AIDS as a Globalizing Panic." In *Global Culture: Nationalism, Globalization and Modernity.* Ed. Mike Featherstone. London: Sage.

O'Neill, Jennifer. 1999. "Cup Switch Paves Way for Male Domination." *Times* (10 December), n.p.

Open the Box: Take the Money and Run. . 1986. Directed by Mike Dibb; script by Jane Root. Videotape. British Film Institute.

Oram at Large. 1990. "Tina's Team's a $2m Turn-On." *Sunday Telegraph* (14 January), 8–9.

"Out of Bounds: Pro-Sports Leagues and Domestic Violence." 1996. *Harvard Law Review* 109, no. 5: 1048–65.

"Out in the Open." 1999. *Village Voice* (9 February), 174.

Page, D. 1997. "Good Guys, Bad Guys." *Rugby League Week*, vol. 28, no. 22 (9 July), 16–17.

Palmer, Rod. 1997. "Interview with Ian Roberts." *Life Matters*, ABC Radio National (June).

Paretsky, Sara. 1995. *Windy City Blues: V. I. Warshawski Stories.* New York: Dell.

Park, Roberta J. 1994. "A Decade of the Body: Researching and Writing about the History of Health, Fitness, Exercise, and Sport, 1983–1993." *Journal of Sport History* 21, no. 1: 59–82.

Patel, N. 1999. "Letter to the Editor." *Toronto Star* (18 February), n.p.

Pearce, Melissa, and Bronwyn Campbell. 1993. "Breaking the Rules." *B and T,* vol. 43, no. 1928, 18–19.

Pela, R. L. 1997. "Big Guy, Small Story." *The Advocate* (2 September), 64–65.

Pener, Degen. 1994. "The Games Men Play." *Gay Games IV Official Souvenir Program,* 26–30.

Penner, Mike. 1999. "Success of the '99 Women's World Cup Is . . . Looking Good." *Los Angeles Times* (8 July), D1.

Pereira, J. 1996. "Fila Scores on an Assist from Grant Hill." *Wall Street Journal* (5 November), B1, B6.

Peters, Roy. 1976. *Television Coverage of Sport.* Birmingham, U.K.: Centre for Contemporary Cultural Studies.

Pichler, D., and Greg Louganis. 1997. "Taking the Plunge." *The Advocate,* no. 739–40 (19 August), 22–31.

Pitts, Brenda G. 1997. "From Leagues of Their Own to an Industry of Their Own: The Emerging Lesbian Sports Industry." *Women in Sport and Physical Activity Journal* 6: 119–39, 165–77.

Pope, Harrison G., Jr., Katharine A. Phillips, and Roberto Olivardia. 2000. *The Adonis Complex: The Secret Crisis of Male Body Obsession.* New York: Free Press.

"Pound Doesn't Get It." 1999. *Toronto Star* (11 March), n.p.

"Power Players." 1999. *Vogue 100* (July), n.p.

Poynton, Beverley, and John Hartley. 1990. "Male-Gazing: Australian Rules Football, Gender and Television." Pp. 144–57 in *Television and Women's Culture: The Politics of the Popular.* Ed. Mary Ellen Brown. Sydney: Currency Press.

Price, S. L. 1999. "Bonus Baby." *Sports Illustrated for Women* (Fall), 86–90.

Pronger, Brian. 1990. *The Arena of Masculinity: Sports, Homosexuality, and the Meaning of Sex.* New York: St. Martin's Press.

———. 1998. "Post-Sport: Transgressing Boundaries in Physical Culture." Pp. 277–98 in *Sport and Postmodern Times.* Ed. Geneviève Rail. Albany: State University of New York Press.

"Protestors Greet Tyson in London." 2000. *New York Times* (17 January), D9.

Pucin, Diane. 1999. "Difference in This Case Is Striking." *Los Angeles Times* (24 December), D1.

Randall, Colin. 1999. "Class Warfare Is the Key to Soccer 'Gay Taunts' Row." *Daily Telegraph* (4 March), 14.

Rasmusson, Erika. 1999–2000. "Strong Signals." *Sports Illustrated for Women* (Winter–Spring), 31–3.

Rawlings, S. 1993. "Luring the Big Boys." *B and T,* vol. 43, no. 1923 (12 February), 18–19.

Reed, Susan. 1994. "Unlevel Playing Fields." Pp. 20–24 in *Gay Games IV Official Souvenir Program.*

Reichert, Tom, Jacqueline Lambiase, Susan Morgan, Meta Carstarphen, and Susan Zavoina. 1999. "Cheesecake and Beefcake: No Matter How You Slice it, Sexual Explicitness in Advertising Continues to Increase." *Journalism and Mass Communication Quarterly* 76, no. 1: 7–20.

Reilly, Rick. 2000. "Bare in Mind." *Sports Illustrated* (4 September), n.p.

Remnick, David. 1996. "Inside-Out Olympics." *New Yorker,* vol. 72, no. 22, 26–8.

Roberts, Ian. 1997. "Foreword." Pp. ix–x in Paul Freeman, *Ian Roberts: Finding Out.* Sydney: Random House.

Roberts, Selena. 1999. "Mauresmo Continues Rise from Nowhere." *New York Times* (4 September), D5.

Rodman, Dennis, with Tim Keown. 1996. *Bad as I Wanna Be.* New York: Bantam.

Rodman, Dennis, with Michael Silver. 1997. *Walk on the Wild Side.* New York: Bantam.

Rogers, Martin. 2000. "Come Out and Play." *Mirror* (18 November), 59.

Rogers, Susan Fox. 1994. "Introduction." Pp. xiii–xvii in *SportsDykes: Stories from On and Off the Field.* Ed. Susan Fox Rogers. New York: St. Martin's Press.

Ross, Andrew. 1998. *Real Love: In Pursuit of Cultural Justice.* New York: New York University Press.

Roveré, A. 1990. "Tough Guys and . . . Imposters." *Rugby League Week,* vol. 21, no. 4 (28 February), 3.

Rowe, David. 1994. "Accommodating Bodies: Celebrity, Sexuality and 'Tragic Magic.'" *Journal of Sport and Social Issues* 18, no. 1: 6–26.

———. 1997a. "Apollo Undone: The Sports Scandal." In *Media Scandals: Morality and Desire in the Popular Culture Marketplace.* Ed. James Lull and S. Hinerman. Cambridge: Polity Press.

———. 1997b. "Big Defence: Sport and Hegemonic Masculinity." Pp. 123–33 in *Gender, Sport and Leisure: Continuities and Challenges.* Ed. Alan Tomlinson. Aachen: Meyer and Meyer Verlag.

Rowe, David, and Peter Brown. 1994. "Promoting Women's Sport: Theory, Policy and Practice." *Leisure Studies* 13, no. 2: 97–110.

Rowe, David, and Geoffrey Lawrence. 1986. "Saluting the State: Nationalism and the Olympics." Pp. 196–203 in *Power Play: Essays in the Sociology of Australian Sport.* Ed. Geoffrey Lawrence and David Rowe. Sydney: Hale and Iremonger.

Rutenberg, Jim, and Stuart Elliott. 2000. "Advertiser Shuns Talk Show as Gay Protest Gains Power." *New York Times* (19 May), A21.

Ryan, B. 1992. "The Two and Only." *Sports Illustrated* (14 December), 46.

Ryan, Joan. 1996. *Little Girls in Pretty Boxes.* New York: Warner Books.

Sabo, Donald. 1993. "Sociology of Sport and New World Disorder." *Sport Science Review* 2, no. 1: 1–9.

Sabo, Donald, and Sue Curry Jansen. 1992. "Images of Men in Sport Media: The Social Reproduction of Gender Order." Pp. 169–84 in

Men, Masculinity, and the Media. Ed. Steve Craig. Newbury Park, Calif.: Sage.

Sacks, Harvey. 1995. *Lectures on Conversation*. Ed. Gail Jefferson. Oxford: Basil Blackwell.

Sage, George H. 1998. *Power and Ideology in American Sport: A Critical Perspective*, 2nd ed. Champaign, Ill.: Human Kinetics Press.

Sailes, Gary A. 1996–97. "Betting Against the Odds: An Overview of Black Sports Participation." *Journal of African American Men* 2, no. 2–3: 11–22.

Sandomir, Richard. 1999. "Women's Soccer Team Won't Go to Australia." *New York Times* (23 December), D1–D2.

Sandoz, Joli. 1995. "Lesbian Sport Fiction." *Lesbian Review of Fiction* 1 (June): 22.

Sargenti, S. L, Dolf Zillman, and J. B. Weaver III. 1998. "The Gender Gap in the Enjoyment of Televised Sports." *Journal of Sport and Social Issues* 22, no. 1: 46–64.

"Sauna Rejects Fashanu Story Cash." 1998. *Pink Paper* (8 May), 1.

Savan, Leslie. 1994. *The Sponsored Life: Ads, TV, and American Culture*. Philadelphia: Temple University Press.

Schaap, Dick. 1994. "Decathlete, Family Man, Games Founder." Pp. 32–3 in *Gay Games IV Official Souvenir Program*.

Schinto, J. 1994. "Narrow World of Sports." *Women's Review of Books* 11, no. 1 (February): 24–5.

Schreier, Barbara A. 1989. "Sporting Wear." Pp. 92–123 in *Men and Women: Dressing the Part*. Ed. Claudia Brush Kidwell and Valerie Steele. Washington, D.C.: Smithsonian Institution Press.

Schulze, Laurie. 1990. "On the Muscle." Pp. 59–78 in *Fabrications: Costume and the Female Body*. Ed. Jane Gaines and Charlotte Herzog. London: Routledge.

Schwartz, H. L. 1997. "Out of Bounds." *The Advocate*, no. 729 (18 March), 56–9.

"Scoring with Wilt." 1999. *Sports Illustrated* (25 October), 38.

Scraton, Sheila. 1987. "'Boys Muscle in Where Angels Fear to Tread'— Girls' Sub-Cultures and Physical Activities." Pp. 160–86 in *Sport, Leisure and Social Relations*. Ed. John Horne, David Jary, and Alan Tomlinson. London: Routledge and Kegan Paul.

Seabrook, Jeremy. 1997. "Tackling the Competition." *New Yorker* (18 August), 42–51.

Shapiro, Michael J. 1989. "Representing World Politics: The Sport/War Intertext." Pp. 69–96 in *International/Intertextual Relations: Postmodern Readings of World Politics*. Ed. James Der Derian and Michael J. Shapiro. Lexington, Ken.: Lexington.

Shilling, Chris. 1991. "Educating the Body: Physical Capital and the Production of Social Inequalities." *Sociology* 25, no. 4: 653–74.

———. 1993. *The Body and Social Theory.* London: Sage.

———. 1994. Review of *Body Matters. Sociological Review* 42, no. 1: 143–5.

Shoebridge, Neil. 1989. "League's New Tack Wins Converts." *Business Review Weekly,* vol. 11, no. 40, 164, 167.

Simmons, T. 1997. "Out at the Olympics." *The Advocate,* no. 724–5 (21 January), 44–6.

Simson, V., and Andrew Jennings. 1992. *The Lords of the Rings: Power, Money and Drugs in the Modern Olympics.* London: Simon and Schuster.

"*SIview.*" 1999.*Sports Illustrated* (8 September), n.p.

Skillen, Anthony. 1993. "Sport: An Historical Phenomenology." *Philosophy* 68, no. 265: 343–68.

Sleeman, R. 1990. "Tina: What's Sport Got to Do with It?" *Australian Magazine* (10–11 March), 8–14.

Sloan, L. 1994. "Taking up Space." Pp. 95–8 in *SportsDykes: Stories from On and Off the Field.* Ed. Susan Fox Rogers. New York: St. Martin's Press.

Sloop, John M. 1997. "Mike Tyson and the Perils of Discursive Constraints: Boxing, Race, and the Assumption of Guilt." Pp. 102–22 in *Out of Bounds: Sports, Media, and the Politics of Identity.* Ed. Aaron Baker and Todd Boyd. Bloomington: Indiana University Press.

Smith, Gary. 2000. "In Love and War." *Sports Illustrated* (2 October), 91–95.

Smith, Paul. 1996. "Acknowledgements." P. ix in *Boys: Masculinities in Contemporary Culture.* Ed. Paul Smith. New York: Westview Press.

Smith, Susan. 1999. "They Call Me Coach: The Women Who Dare to Lead Men into Battle." *Village Voice* (27 April), 76.

Smith, Timothy W. 1999. "When (Heavyweight) Words Collide." *New York Times* (11 March), D2.

"SOCC: Union Boss Slams Fowler Apology." 1999. *AAP Sports News* (7 March), n.p.

Solomon, Alisa. 1994. "Queer Culture: A Celebration—and a Critique." *Village Voice* (21 June), 3–4.

Solomon, Alisa, Michael Eskenazi, and Joanna Cagan. 1999. "Jockbeat." *Village Voice* (8 June), 189.

Sparks, Robert. 1992. "'Delivering the Male': Sports, Canadian Television, and the Making of TSN." *Canadian Journal of Communication* 17, no. 1: 319–42.

Spence, S. N.d. Web site. Available from: www.allaustralian.com/ stuartspeance/duncanar.html.

Spencer, Nancy E. 1997. "Once Upon a Subculture: Professional Women's Tennis and the Meaning of Style, 1970–1974." *Journal of Sport and Social Issues* 21, no. 4: 363–78.

Spitzack, Carole. 1998. "The Production of Masculinity in Interpersonal Communication." *Communication Theory* 8, no. 2: 143–64.

"Sport from the Settee." 1995. *Spectrum*, no. 18 (Summer), 24.

Stanley, J. 1977. "Paradigmatic Woman: The Prostitute." In *Papers in Language Variation*, ed. D. Shores and C. Hines. University of Alabama Press.

"Stars Raced on 'No Test' Agreement." 1998. *Independent* (5 August), n.p.

Stein, Joel. 1999. "Only His Hairdresser Knows for Sure." *Time* (19 July), 78.

Steiner, Wendy. 2000. "Lost in Amazonia." *The Nation* (15 May), 25–30.

Stockwell, A., and J. V. McAuley. 1996. "Tackling the NFL Closet." *The Advocate*, no. 723 (24 December), 51–5.

Stoddart, Brian. 1986. *Saturday Afternoon Fever: Sport in Australian Culture*. Sydney: Angus and Robertson.

"Stopping Steroid Abuse." 1999. *Sports Illustrated for Women* (Fall), 26.

Stratton, Jon. 1986. "Australia—This Sporting Life." Pp. 85–114 in *Power Play: Essays in the Sociology of Australian Sport*. Ed. Geoffrey Lawrence and David Rowe. Sydney: Hale and Iremonger.

Sullivan, Robert. 1999. "Goodbye to Heroin Chic. Now It's Sexy to Be Strong." *Time* (19 July), 62.

Swift, E. M. 1991. "Dangerous Games." *Sports Illustrated* (18 November), 40–3.

Taslitz, Andrew E. 1996. "Patriarchal Stories I: Cultural Rape Narratives in the Courtroom." *California Review of Law and Women's Studies* 5.

"TEN: French Lesbian Group Supports Tennis star Mauresmo." 1999. AAP Sports News (4 February), n.p.

"TEN: Stevenson Hits the Headlines." 1999. AAP Sports News (1 July), n.p.

"There's Life Outside Sports. There's Also Ballet." 1998. *Broadcasting and Cable* (11 May), 24–5.

Thévenin, Patrick. 1997. "Ian Roberts." *Têtu*, no. 18 (October), n.p.

Thompson, Shona. 1999. *Mother's Taxi: Sport and Women's Labor*. Albany: State University of New York Press.

Tien, Ellen. 1999. "The More Hairless Ape." *New York Times* (20 June), 3.

"A Time to Remember." 1998. *Axiom News* (10 September), 4.

Tomlinson, Alan, and Ilkay Yorganci. 1997. "Male Coach/Female Athlete Relations: Gender and Power Relations in Competitive Sport." *Journal of Sport and Social Issues* 21, no. 2: 134–55.

Treichler, Paula. 1987. "AIDS, Homophobia and Biomedical Discourse: An Epidemic of Signification." *Cultural Studies* 1: 263–305.

————. 1988. "AIDS, Gender and Biomedical Discourse: Current Contests for Meaning." In *AIDS: The Burden of History.* Ed. E. Fee and D. Fox. Berkeley: University of California Press.

————. 1999. *How to Have Theory in an Epidemic: Cultural Chronicles of AIDS.* Durham, N.C.: Duke University Press.

Trujillo, N. 1991. "Hegemonic Masculinity on the Mound: Media Representations of Nolan Ryan and American Sports Culture." *Critical Studies in Mass Communication* 8: 240–308.

Tudor, Andrew. 1992. "Them and Us: Story and Stereotype in TV World Cup Coverage." *European Journal of Communication* 7, no. 3: 391–413.

Tuggle, Charles A. 1999. "Differences in Television Sports Reporting of Men's and Women's Athletics: ESPN *SportsCenter* and CNN *Sports Tonight.*" *Journal of Broadcasting and Electronic Media* 41, no. 1: 14–24.

Tuggle, Charles A., and Anne Owen. 1999. "A Descriptive Analysis of NBC's Coverage of the Centennial Olympics: The 'Games of the Woman'?" *Journal of Sport and Social Issues* 23, no. 2: 171–82.

"Two Horses Beat Johnson, Muscle Car Doesn't." 1998. Reuters (16 October).

"Tyson Released Early from Jail for Good Behavior." 1999. *New York Times* (25 May), D8.

US Open Tennis Magazine. 1999.

Van Tiggelen, John. 1999. "Caught in the Slips." *Good Weekend* (22 May), 22–6.

Vannier, M., and H. B. Poindexter. 1960. *Individual and Team Sports for Girls and Women.* Philadelphia: W. B. Saunders.

Vecsey, George. 1999. "Americans Still Dine Together." *New York Times* (8 July), D1.

Verhovek, Sam Howe. 1999. "When a Man Meets a Woman (in the Ring)." *New York Times* (3 October), 24.

Villarosa, Linda. 1994. "Gay Games IV." Pp. 17–19 in *Gay Games IV Official Souvenir Program.*

Vines, Gail. 1988. "Is Sport Good for Children?" *New Scientist,* vol. 119, no. 1022, 46–57.

Voepel, Mechelle. 1999. "Does Soccer Need Sex Appeal?" *Kansas City Star* (8 July), D1.

Volkerling, Michael. 1994. "Death or Transfiguration: The Future for Cultural Policy in New Zealand." *Culture and Policy* 6, no. 1: 7–28.

Wahl, G., and L. J. Wertheim. 1998. "Paternity Ward." *Sports Illustrated,* vol. 88, no. 18, 62–71.

Walker, Sam. 1999. "Big Sponsors Snub Women's Tennis." *Wall Street Journal* (1 July), B1, B12.

Wallace, Michele. 1991. *Black Macho and the Myth of the Superwoman.* London: Verso.

Watson, Rod. 1973. "The Public Announcement of Fatality." *Working Papers in Cultural Studies*, no. 4, 5–20.

Watson-Smyth, Kate. 1998. "Fear of Arrest Led Fashanu Hanging Himself." *Independent* (10 September), 9.

Weidler, Dannt. 1999. "Sparks Fly in Roberts–Jack Feud." *Sun-Herald* Internet edition (21 March). Available from: www.sunherald.com.au/content/19990321/sports/sport_story1.html.

Weir, T. 1999. "Revelation Can Often Take a Toll. Mauresmo Faces Scrutiny On, Off the Court." *USA Today* (4 February), 3C.

Wells, Jeff. 1991. "Fire Them Up Fred, Before They Go to Pot." *Weekend Australian* (16–17 November), 70.

Wenner, Lawrence A. 1993. "Intersections as Dangerous Places: Theories and Role Models in Sport Studies." *Journal of Sport and Social Issues* 17, no. 2: 75–6.

———. 1998. "In Search of the Sports Bar: Masculinity, Alcohol, Sports, and the Mediation of Public Space." Pp. 302–32 in *Sport and Postmodern Times*. Ed. Geneviève Rail. Albany: State University of New York Press.

Wenner, Lawrence A., and Walter Gantz. 1998. "Watching Sports on Television: Audience Experience, Gender, Fanship, and Marriage." Pp. 233–51 in *MediaSport*. Ed. Lawrence A. Wenner. London: Routledge.

West, P. 1997. "This Is a Man's Man's World." *Weekend Australian* (5–6 July), 8.

Wetherell, Margaret, and Nigel Edley. 1999. "Negotiating Hegemonic Masculinity: Imaginary Positions and Psycho-Discursive Practices." *Feminism and Psychology* 9, no. 3: 335–56.

Whannel, Gary. 1999. "Sports Stars, Narrativization and Masculinities." *Leisure Studies* 18, no. 3: 249–65.

Wheeler, David L. 1999. "Could Boys Get 'Barbie Syndrome'?" *Chronicle of Higher Education* (11 June), A22.

"White Appears in Anti-Homosexual Ad." 1998. *Greensboro News and Record* (22 July), 2144.

White, P., and J. Gillett. 1994. "Reading the Muscular Body: A Critical Decoding of Advertisements in *Flex* Magazine." *Sociology of Sport Journal* 11, no. 1: 18–39.

Wieland, Jake. 1993. "Sports Shorts." *St. Louis Post-Dispatch* (6 February), 2C.

Wilkins, Peter. 1996. "The Tough League." Pp. 198–202 in *League of a Nation*. Ed. David Headon and Lex Marinos. Sydney: ABC Books.

Williams, Lena. 2000. "Women Play More, but Coach Less." *New York Times* (3 May), D8.

Williams, Richard. 1999. "Both These Footballers Are at the Pinnacle of Their Profession." *Independent* (4 March), 1.

Williamson, Judith. 1988. "AIDS and Perceptions of the Grim Reaper." *Metro*, no. 80, 2–6.

"Woman Beats Man in Boxing Gender Bender." 1999. *Daily Illini* (11 October), 23.

Woog, Dan. 1998. *Jocks: True Stories of America's Gay Male Athletes*. Los Angeles: Alyson.

Wright, Jan. 1991. "Gracefulness and Strength: Sexuality in the Seoul Olympics." *Social Semiotics* 1, no. 1: 49–66.

Young, J. 1999. "Mauresmo Creates a PR Problem." *Washington Times* (5 February), B6.

Young, Kevin. 1997. "Women, Sport and Physicality: Preliminary Findings from a Canadian Study." *International Review for the Sociology of Sport* 32: 297–305.

Youngblood, Kent. 1998. "White Is Tight-Lipped after Smith's Blasts." *Wisconsin State Journal* (7 August), 1B.

Zimet, J. 1994. "Confessions of a Confirmed Couch Potato, or, the Lamentations of a Latent Sports Dyke." Pp. 111–17 in *SportsDykes: Stories from On and Off the Field*. Ed. Susan Fox Rogers. New York: St. Martin's Press.

Zwerman, G. 1995. *Martina Navratilova*. New York: Chelsea House.

Index